From
Trauma
to
Leadership

Making Your Trauma Purposeful

Selena Veach

Copyright © 2025 by Selena Veach

All rights reserved.

No portion of this book may be reproduced in any form without written permission from the publisher or author, except as permitted by U.S. copyright law.

Contents

Dedication	1
Introduction	3
Chapter 1 My Journey and Learning to Forgive	9
Chapter 2 Evaluating Our Beliefs	23
Chapter 3 Reframing Our Beliefs with Truth	39
Chapter 4 Learning to Live in Truth	57
Chapter 5 Giving Compassion	71
Chapter 6 Embracing Courage	89
Chapter 7 Learning to Pivot	105
Chapter 8 Persistence and Endurance	121

Chapter 9 Inner Health and Strength	139
Chapter 10 Learning to Lead	157
Chapter 11 The New You as a Leader	173
Appendix A	189
Acknowledgements	193
Let's Stay Connected!	195
References	197

"Thereafter, Hagar used another name to refer to the Lord, who had spoken to her. She said, 'You are the God who sees me.' She also said, 'Have I truly seen the One who sees me?'" (Ge. 16:13)

"'For I know the plans I have for you,' says the Lord. 'They are plans for good and not for disaster, to give you a future and a hope. In those days when you pray, I will listen. If you look for me wholeheartedly, you will find me. I will be found by you,' says the Lord." (Je. 29:11-12)

To my dear ones who have suffered much,

God has seen you, and he knows your heart. He has more in store for you, he will continue to give you a future and a hope.

Introduction

I had spent too many years in a wilderness mentality. I had always wondered why it took the Israelites so long to reach the Promised Land. How could you spend forty years wandering about, when it should have been an eleven-day journey? Until I realized I too was an Israelite.

Twenty-five years of making the same choices and mistakes. Too many years staying stuck in what I knew wasn't "great" but felt "manageable." I knew how to cope. I assumed this was what everyone else's life was like. It wasn't what I had hoped for out of my life, but at the root of it I didn't believe I deserved better. I kept complaining about it and being frustrated by it, but I was unwilling to make a choice to change.

But we all have a tipping point. I didn't want to die in the desert. I wanted to see the Promised Land. For me, that point came when what had started as a not-perfect relationship turned into a toxic one, and it pushed me over the edge. No relationship is perfect or easy. But some are not only too hard to accept but will slowly kill you.

I bet you can relate. You too have probably reached that tipping point in your own life. Whether you wished for it or not, your trauma pushed you into a choice. You could choose not to face the problem and continue your fight-or-flight response every time an issue comes up. You could choose to hide behind your emotions and be an angry, hurt, defensive person.

But you chose differently. You chose to heal, to forgive, to start again. It may have been purely for your own survival, but you made the choice. For that you can be thankful. Your trauma pushed you to your breaking point, so you chose to survive rather than give in. That process brought you to your healing.

Looking for More

For me, the healing process felt like a painful sacrifice. And yet, so worth it to stop making the same mistakes. I needed to know it meant something, that everything I lost or gave up was to get me to a better place, somewhere where I could still impact the lives of people around me.

Maybe you feel that way too—that the enormity of your suffering looks incredulous from an outside perspective. We know what happened to us isn't our fault, but we need it to have meaning.

If you have started your healing journey but still feel like it was all worthless, I'm here to tell you that it's not. You gained strengths as you've recovered. You've grown in wisdom and in character. And, God can use these strengths to share with or teach others. I don't think our creator limits us to simply healing. He *creates*, even out of brokenness. I believe he has more for us. A story to tell, a gift to share, a way to influence those around us for his good.

Defining Trauma

Let's spend just a minute defining trauma. By picking up this book, I'm assuming either you've experienced trauma or someone close to you has. Trauma refers to your response following an event that psychologically overwhelms you, often resulting in shock, denial, and changes in the body, mind, and behavior.

Trauma is typically associated with significant events such as physical or sexual assault, violence, or accidents. But it can also involve responses to repeated events, like ongoing emotional abuse or childhood neglect.

Trauma that repeatedly occurs over time can have a cumulative impact. This is known as complex trauma. Early experiences of trauma can leave a deep imprint on your worldview, sense of self, and relationships later in life (Ryder, 2025)[1].

As you'll see from my story, the type of trauma I am most familiar with is relationship trauma. My trauma included emotional and mental abuse both by people close to me and in authority over me, neglect, religious trauma, and an overly strict upbringing. I've experienced complex trauma, having endured some portions of my abuse since childhood.

I can't speak with experience over most acute trauma, so please consider my teaching to be broadly applicable for those scenarios.

---

1. Ryder, G. (2025, February 18). *Psych Central*. Retrieved from https://psychcentral.com/health/what-is-trauma

Moving Forward Together

After healing from trauma, we run the risk of settling in life, never wanting to explore or engage again. We accept not exposing ourselves to potential trauma as enough. We have suffered, it's reasonable to want to stay safe. Setting up good boundaries and establishing healthy relationships in our lives should be our first focus to feel that safety.

As I healed, I did that, but I still felt unsettled. Maybe you are too. I needed someone and something in my life, a way to give back to the people around me and center myself in a community. I asked God for more, for meaning and purpose.

As we move forward together, I want to help you see who you are in Christ, and then see how the trauma and pain you've experienced have helped develop character traits that make you into a strong leader. Then we'll talk about what stepping into leadership looks like in your life.

Once you see these characteristics in yourself, you'll see you can do more than survive your trauma. You'll be able to thrive again—or maybe for the first time. Your strength is not lost to those who held you back, hurt you, and took away your love for yourself. Your strength is deep within you and now refined.

What Leadership can Look Like

What does leadership look like for you? We often think of leadership in a work environment or with a large organization, but that's not the only places we find it. Leadership can sound intimidating, but I want to help you see where you're already a leader or where it would be easy for you to start. Let's look at some examples together.

Let's look at your family first. If you're a parent, godparent, even an involved aunt or uncle, you're already a leader. Part of your role as a parent is to be a role model to your children. You're teaching them all the "firsts" when they're little, helping them to learn. You're guiding them as they mature into children who can interact in groups. You help them understand what they're learning in school, possibly tutoring them in areas where they're struggling.

As teens you're coaching them on how to take on responsibility, how to handle their emotions, and how to persevere towards their goals. As young adults you're setting them up for success on their own. You continue to mentor and support them as they take on new challenges as adults. Throughout their lives, you've discipled them in God's Word and given them the example of worshipping together as a family.

Those things may sound like the normal things most parents do. What you're not seeing there is all the skills you're using as a leader. You're a role model; you're teaching and tutoring. You're coaching, mentoring, and supporting. You're discipling. All these words describe a leader.

In your community are you already involved in supporting an organization you believe in? Are you helping them fundraise or supporting events and activities for the community to be involved in? Are you helping change policies for the betterment of the community you live in? All these things are leadership as well.

If you're involved in your local church, what does that look like? Are you organizing events, are you leading a small group, a life group, or a Bible study? Are you teaching children, youth, or women? Are you leading a portion of the ministry? Do you speak at events?

All these things and many more are leadership. You're already a leader, you just haven't defined it that way. Often, we feel leadership has to be big—impacting or leading large numbers of people. But it doesn't start that way. Don't be afraid of small beginnings. Our ministry and our impact will grow in the time and space God has for it; it's our role to stay open to his leading.

The world needs to experience your character and strength. You'll see where you can use these traits to serve and lead in your home and community. Your words matter, your experience matters, and you didn't survive and fight for your healing to remain hidden.

God wants to use you to encourage others, to show them the path out of their own trauma. You can help give them the steps to start anew in their own lives.

Let's take that walk together. I'll tell you some of my story and how I learned forgiveness. Then I want to help you re-center your beliefs on truth and see your experiences with a new vision. As you hear my story, think about your own experiences that helped form your beliefs.

Chapter 1
My Journey and Learning to Forgive

I believe God brought us together because he knew I could relate to some of the things you've been through and find some of my experiences or learning helpful. I'll share a little bit of my story, so we can get to know each other. Think of this like tea or coffee with a new friend. Let's get comfortable and settle in for a good friendship journey.

A Bit About Me

I'm your small-town American girl who grew up on a fifteen-acre hobby farm in rural western Oregon. My parents had both grown up on farms and believed it was the best way to teach us strong values, so they purchased a small farm when I was seven. We were about ten miles outside of town.

My mom was raised in a Baptist church, and we grew up in that same church. The church was a small rural farming community church with great people and very conservative roots. This was also in the era where salvation was often offered as a fear-based proposition, with a helping of "God loves you" served up as a healthy side dish.

My parents came with their own stories. My dad did two tours in Vietnam early in their marriage. He had been a quiet but fun-loving and mischievous character. He came back a quiet, somber adult who'd seen too much tragedy for him to process.

When I was a kid, my mom was my Brownie leader and 4-H leader, teaching me to cook, sew, learn new hobbies, and how to go on adventures. She was fun-loving and active, a lively friend and a co-conspirator for mischief.

During my teenage years, my mom started having many health issues, which required several surgeries. I was faced with adult responsibilities at a young age to keep the family unit functioning. The recovery from the surgeries got my mom addicted to painkillers, and she was unable to ever completely kick the habit.

My fun-loving mom turned into a manipulative and controlling addict, who abandoned me emotionally in the years when I needed her most. I believe her own mother spoke fear and shame over her life, and she translated that into terrible self-worth. The combination of shame and lack of control shaped her beliefs and promoted the development of the narcissist in her personality.

I started my career during and after college, managing kitchens at Christian conference centers, preparing meals for 125-250 guests at a time. It was a very active and somewhat stressful job, but I loved it. It was my passion to serve people meals they would enjoy and relieve them from the burden of meal planning and preparation so they could focus on what they were learning instead.

I loved the combination of work, creativity, and ministry all rolled into one. I got to minister to guests, as well as to both my summer and year-round staff. The work required long, tiring hours, but the rewards were many. My first manager is still the best manager I've worked for. I'll share more about her later when we talk through leadership examples.

I met my first husband when he attended a retreat at the conference center where I worked in Colorado. He was a new Christian and on fire for God. He was an active skier and surfer and enjoyed most outdoor activities. We spent our dating time getting to know each other through outdoor adventures.

He was also a recovering alcoholic. Unfortunately, it was only a year into our marriage that he first relapsed. The alcoholic in him was manipulative and deceitful. I supported him through a lot of mistakes and multiple drug and alcohol treatment programs. Later, he needed multiple surgeries, where he became re-addicted to painkillers. The addict became the dominant character in his life.

After several hard years, we looked for opportunities for my husband to get a fresh start. I took a new job in another state, and we packed up our lives. I moved ahead of him. But without me there to keep things together for him, my husband lost his job and relapsed again. He fell into a deep depression.

In my new town, I met a woman through a mutual friend in a similar situation to mine. I noticed she wore a small bottle on a necklace. She explained to me that it contained her husband's prescriptions for the day, and the rest were locked in a safe at home that he didn't have access to.

She would dole out his medication to him at the appropriate time because he couldn't be trusted to be responsible with it himself. I saw my future flash before my eyes. I was ten years into this marriage, and my husband had struggled with his addictions for all but the first year. He wasn't ready or willing to change.

This was who I would be if I stayed in this marriage, and I couldn't do it. I didn't want to be that person. I begged God to release me from my commitment. I struggled for a long time over whether divorce was a choice I could make. But when he chose to relapse again the day we miscarried, I told him to leave.

I was so beaten down from the constant lies and manipulation of an alcoholic/addict in my first husband that I was weak and easy prey for a narcissist. It wasn't long before one found me. The love bombing won me over and I was hooked. We married a year later.

My second husband and I did a lot of outdoor activities and some travel; this is where I fell in love with backpacking. But I wasn't happy at home. There, I faced verbal, mental, and emotional manipulation and abuse.

After ten years invested in this relationship, I had lost who I was. I was constantly walking on eggshells around his anger, always making sure everything was taken care of to try to avoid another outburst. He always thought the worst of everyone, and I was often the source of his blame.

Like many of us caught in a cycle of abuse, I stayed for the good days, even though there were few. I tried. I really tried. But I finally had to admit he was never going to change.

I had again believed in the fantasy of who someone said they wanted to be instead of evaluating the reality of who they were. When I realized I had lost myself, lost my chance for my own children, lost the relationship with his kids, and saw a future that continued only to feed his addictions and ego, I saw what I had chosen ten years earlier. I realized I had to make a different choice.

It wasn't just that he wouldn't change. I had allowed myself to completely change who I was to appease him. I couldn't allow that for myself any longer either. I could no longer live under the control of a man who only had his own best interests at heart, and I couldn't accept the loss of myself. I chose to walk away.

> This was the moment that courage took hold in my life. I had finally learned I was worth fighting for. It was time to change my ways.

Recognition

Let me take a minute to pause and say, if you do relate to these stories, I hope there were people in your life you could lean on. I recognize that's not usually the case, which can make us feel trapped and as if we don't have a way out of a bad situation.

If you can relate, I want you to know I'm sorry for what happened to you. I understand how this happens, and I was there too. I know it often doesn't make sense to someone looking in from the outside, but for those of us who have been there, it can be so easy to lose yourself in the situation.

Moving Towards Healing

I spent the pandemic working with a great counselor. She combined chakra with prayer and forgiveness. Stay with me here, I realize it sounds a bit "out there," but it was effective. The theory for correlating chakra with your emotional and spiritual healing is that your body also physically stores the memories of your trauma and can hinder your ability to heal.

In a session with her, we would spend some time talking about what feelings or issues were triggering me most that day. I would speak forgiveness over whomever I needed to forgive for that scenario—whether it was myself, someone else, or what I had believed about God at that moment.

Don't get me wrong, most of the time I didn't want to forgive someone, yet, but I believed in the power of releasing those emotions and turning them over to God. My forgiveness was out of obedience, not out of how I was feeling. I would repeat the words of forgiveness three times for each person.

Then we would concentrate on what emotions I was feeling and correlate which areas of the body were holding those emotions. I would spend a few minutes visualizing the memory of that trauma while holding a hand over my head or my heart, depending on the specific feelings. Then I would visualize letting go of those emotions and forgiving them.

We would pray together to renounce those emotions and feelings and lay them at the feet of Jesus. I would release my hold on my emotions and fears. We allowed God to pour over me forgiveness and asked him to replace those emotions with a healthy one; for example, replacing my anger and grief around being manipulated with freedom and strength from the Holy Spirit. She also taught me tapping exercises where I could repeat mantras to myself to reframe my beliefs—saying to myself, "My subconscious admits I have a right to put down boundaries and say no."

I didn't realize how much unforgiveness I was holding onto until I walked through this experience. Not only was my body physically telling me it was struggling, but my heart and my mind were stuck in an endless loop trying to work through what I was feeling without being able to let go. I was afraid that if I forgave my offenders, I would be giving them permission to hurt me.

The opposite was true. My unforgiveness wasn't impacting them at all. They had gone on with their lives. I was the one stuck in my grief, anger, and bitterness, overwhelmed by the myriad of emotions I was feeling. My refusing to let go was only hurting me.

This is where I first started learning to give myself compassion for the mistakes I had made. By accepting my own failures, I could begin to have compassion for people around me, realizing their intentions were not always to hurt, but that sometimes they were learning as well.

Today

I'm so thankful for my life today. God has been faithful throughout my story, even when I wasn't very faithful to him. He's always protected me, always provided for me generously, and always been pursuing my heart. He's never given up on me, no matter how long it's taken me to turn back to him.

Once I chose to listen, God put me back on the path he had for me. I moved back to Washington, which is where he had led me to all along. He gave me a beautiful home, my sanctuary from the world, my safe place to continue my healing. I live where I can get out in nature easily, because God's voice is often closest to me when I'm out in his creation.

After many years of chasing the corporate ladder, I was blessed with an opportunity to become a management consultant, where I can teach and advise instead of constantly striving to achieve someone else's goals. God continues to give me opportunities to be involved in women's lives too, teaching and ministering again. He has also been very gracious to provide me with many strong women as good friends and support.

God has turned my life around for the good. I've been willing to take the steps to pivot the direction my life was going. God ignited in me the dream I'm working towards today. This book is a beginning. I want this to be the foundation for a ministry to women who have walked through trauma, stepped into their healing, and want to use what they've learned to lead and minister to others. I want to teach women how to practically apply these steps in their own lives.

I see this in a couple of different forms. This will look like studying together in small groups, online, in churches, and at retreats. But I also want to create a place of refuge for the public to come in and see a different attitude and approach. I want them to know there's somewhere safe they can come and talk with friends and share their hearts.

I also want to provide a space where women can come and work together, while also learning practical skills they can take with them. In my mind this looks like a ministry housed within a bakery. A place to work, a place of refuge, a place to minister and be ministered to. A place that supports the organizations that help women step out of their trauma and provides them with the resources to make better choices.

Forgiveness

Before we can take a journey into health out of our healing, we need to have journeyed through forgiveness. Before we're ready to lead others, we have to allow God to work in our hearts, to reach into the depths of our pain and be willing to let him heal us.

Let me caveat, I'm not saying we need to be done with that journey before we can reach others. But we need to have taken enough time and space to allow him to speak into our lives. Give yourself a year, often two. I know that sounds like forever and can be discouraging, but this is a time to treasure.

God will speak to your heart and strengthen you if you give him the space to do it and are willing to learn. These quiet times can be the sweetest part of your journey if, for a while, you stop striving and allow yourself the time to recover and learn.

Many of us struggle early on in our journey with refusing to forgive those who hurt us. We want them to suffer like we've suffered. We want to withhold forgiveness from them, hoping it hurts them a little bit or at least makes them recognize what they've done.

We feel justified in our anger because our pain validates those feelings. We use our anger and pain to build a shielding wall in hopes that we won't get hurt again. We rely only on ourselves because trusting someone else, even God, has led us to pain before.

Unfortunately, when we withhold forgiveness, we only hurt our own hearts. It can make us bitter and angry at not just the people who hurt us, but at the world around us. We transfer that anger and blame to God because he allowed the situations that hurt us. But our response doesn't help anyone, especially not us.

The risk we take by allowing unforgiveness in our lives will give the devil permission to gain a stronghold in our hearts. That unforgiveness easily translates to bitterness, anger, and defensiveness in our lives. Our minds are constantly filled with thoughts about what happened and our emotions surrounding it. And the people who hurt us are not impacted by our unforgiveness.

For our own peace, we have to learn to forgive. The key to forgiveness is our obedience to God's direction, even when our hearts don't feel like it. God has asked us, commanded us, to forgive; therefore, we need to forgive.

Let's look at what his Word says.

- *"If you **forgive** those who sin against you, your heavenly Father will **forgive** you. But if you refuse to forgive others, your Father will not forgive your sins."* Mt. 6:14-15 (NLT)

- *"I tell you, you can pray for anything, and if you believe that you've received it, it will be yours. But when you are praying, first **forgive** anyone you are holding a grudge against, so that your Father in heaven will **forgive** your sins, too."* Mk. 11:24-25 (NLT)

- *"Make allowance for each other's faults, and **forgive** anyone who offends you. Remember, the Lord forgave you, so you must **forgive** others."* Cl. 3:13 (NLT)

We forgive from a place of repentance and desire for wholeness. That doesn't mean we feel like forgiving. I would say often we don't feel like it. But if we wait until we feel like forgiving someone, we never will.

My unforgiveness can lead me into sin. Not only am I disobeying what God has called me to do, but I'm holding on to feelings that lead to resentment and bitterness in my heart. This leads me away from God. If I'm storing up resentment and bitterness, I'm not allowing love and compassion to fill my heart. I have become more cynical.

What I have found is my feelings follow in time when I'm obedient to his direction. My heart and soul let go of the burden I have been carrying in all my anger. By choosing to forgive first, I allow my heart to catch up after the fact, and I feel that I have forgiven those who hurt me.

Forgiveness includes forgiving myself as well. I may not have caused a situation, but I may have said or done things in my hurt that were hurtful as well. I may have clung to anger and defensiveness for a long time to protect myself, rather than choosing to let God heal me.

I may also have taken on their issues as my own. I may have accepted the lies they told me, taking them as truth about me. That's not who God made me to be.

Forgiving those who hurt us and forgiving ourselves are equally important. If I keep holding onto unforgiveness, I lose. If I turn it over to God, he allows me freedom.

I also need to forgive if I want to be able to lead. I can't hold onto my anger and pain like a safety blanket and assume it won't impact my decisions. People will make mistakes and frustrate me along the way. I have to learn to forgive them if I want to continue to work beside them towards a common goal.

Unforgiveness will harbor hurt and pain that interferes with all my relationships: my faith journey, my marriage, my work relationships, my friendships. I'll hold biases and make poor choices if I'm still living out of my pain. I have to forgive so I can learn how to be forgiven.

My forgiveness is what changes my attitude. Instead of approaching the world from a posture of pain, I can approach with humility, knowing I need forgiveness as much as anyone else does. My humility allows my faith to grow, and will make me an approachable leader.

Have you taken the time to forgive those who hurt you? Let's start today to forgive in obedience to God's direction. We can trust him to heal our hearts in the process.

Next, let's look at how our beliefs were formed and evaluate if we need to change them in order to become the faith-filled leader God has set in front of us to become.

Chapter 2
Evaluating Our Beliefs

Doubting God's Goodness

Throughout my young life, I dreamed of getting married and having a family. That was the most important goal portrayed to me by my family. Getting a bachelor's degree was a close second. A degree had to happen before marriage because Mom and Dad had married before they finished college, and then Mom had been unable to complete her degree.

I was the good child; I did the things that were expected of me. I earned a bachelor's degree, then got engaged shortly after graduation. The engagement didn't last, so I earned a second bachelor's degree while my heart healed.

A few years later, I got married. I was not fortunate enough to have children of my own. My husband and I suffered one miscarriage, and our marriage dissolved shortly after. It has taken many years of wrestling with God to begin to understand why I couldn't have that dream.

It was an expectation for me, what would make me "normal" and "accepted." I had staked my self-worth on my ability to have a successful marriage and family. For many years, my heart did not believe in God's goodness because I didn't know how to find my worth in him instead of my successes. I believed I was somehow to blame, unworthy of being given that dream.

These are the kind of moments where we begin to doubt God's goodness. Our heart says, "Lord, how could you do this to me?" We trust him a little less.

Over time, these moments build up. We believe the lie that God must not really love us completely if he gives us desires that are unachievable. The more we see dreams shattered, the cumulative effect becomes overwhelming to our hearts.

Take a moment to remember and write your answers to the following questions:

- How many dreams were shattered in your life?

- Are you overwhelmed by your loss of dreams?

- Have you begun to doubt God's goodness in your life? If so, can you see the moment when you started to doubt God?

I understand how we get to doubting based on what we've seen in our lives, how life doesn't feel fair, or like a good God is orchestrating our lives. But here's where we need to ask ourselves another question. Have we made a choice to doubt?

In John 20:24-29, we see the story of Jesus appearing to Thomas.

> *One of the twelve disciples, Thomas (nicknamed the Twin), was not with the others when Jesus came. They told him, "We have seen the Lord!"*
>
> *But he replied, "I won't believe it unless I see the nail wounds in his hands, put my fingers into them, and place my hand into the wound in his side."*
>
> *Eight days later, the disciples were together again, and this time Thomas was with them. The doors were locked, but suddenly, as before, Jesus was standing among them. "Peace be with you," he said. Then he said to Thomas, "Put your finger here, and look at my hands. Put your hand into the wound in my side. Don't be faithless any longer. Believe!"*
>
> *"My Lord and my God!" Thomas exclaimed.*
>
> *Then Jesus told him, "You believe because you have seen me. Blessed are those who believe without seeing me."*

It's worth noting that when Jesus appeared to the disciples, Thomas was not with them. We're not told why he isn't there, but I have to wonder if he had started doubting in his heart already. When the other disciples tell him they've seen Jesus, his response is that he won't believe until he sees Jesus himself.

It's not that he couldn't believe in God. It was a choice he made. He **won't** believe. It was an active choice, a statement of his will, an act of defiance.

This is where we need to evaluate our own lives, our own choices. Have we chosen to doubt as an act of defiance against God? Are we still angry for the hurt he allowed in our lives? It can be hard to see past the pain. It may be a long time before we can see how our circumstances led us back to God and made us stronger. But God is always working.

Eve

From the beginning, Satan entered our hearts and whispered lies over us. He is the father of lies; he started lying to us in the garden of Eden. Let's go back there for a minute. First, let's look at the instructions given to Adam in Genesis 2:16.

God told Adam he could eat from any tree in the garden except the Tree of Life. If he ate from that tree, he would die. We're not told if God gave the same instructions to Eve or if Adam relayed them to her. But based on her responses to the serpent, she is also aware of this instruction.

The serpent approaches Eve with a twisting of the truth. He asks Eve, "*Did God really say you must not eat the fruit from any of the trees in the garden?*" (Ge. 3:1) He wants her to see God as limiting her, working against her.

He begins to sow the seeds of doubt in her mind. She begins to question if God has her best in mind, or if he would limit her power and knowledge. Her questions hinge on how well she knows God's character.

Has God limited her in anything else up to this point? Rather than remembering that God generously gave them the whole garden to enjoy and only gave them one rule to follow, with Satan twisting God's words in front of her, suddenly, she sees God as limiting instead of generous. This is what manipulation looks like.

Her response to the serpent shows she's falling into Satan's web of deceit. "*Of course, we may eat fruit from the trees in the garden,*" she replies. "*It's only the fruit from the tree in the middle of the garden that we are not allowed to eat. God said, 'You must not eat it or even touch it; if you do, you will die.'*"

Wait, what? When did God say she couldn't *touch* the fruit from the tree in the center of the garden? His instruction was not to *eat* the fruit from the Tree of Life. She's already extended the consequences beyond how they were stated, reflecting the limitation she feels in her heart.

That direction was provided for her good. The consequence of knowing good and evil was death. God was giving her the option for eternal life by being obedient in following one instruction. But she believed the lie Satan set in front of her. She would gain wisdom and be like God if she ate of the fruit.

This is how Satan leads us down the path of sin: with a whisper of truth, told with a lie that plays to our weakness or desires. He was accurate that she would gain understanding by eating the fruit. He just left out the facts of the consequences.

He blatantly tells her she won't die, which is the opposite of what God told her. But she believes him because he's already sown the seed of doubt in her heart by twisting God's words and intentions.

Just like Eve, I believed that God didn't have my best in mind. This is where we all get caught. In our weaknesses, in our doubt of God's character, in our lack of knowledge of the truth. These beliefs lead us down the path to bad choices.

Generational Sin

In my journey to healing, there was another factor I didn't account for. When I walked through my trauma with my counselor, she started in chronological order. So, instead of walking through my ended marriages, the first item we addressed was family history—how my family members' stories and beliefs had impacted my life. What I found was a history of shame.

Shame that had been passed down through generations of women in my family. A history of women who needed to perform to earn their redemption because they had been taught they were unworthy. A history of women who didn't know how to instill unconditional love into their own children because they had not learned it from their parents.

> I firmly believe the words we speak over each other have meaning and influence. For good or for bad.

We can take them too lightly or not think about the impact they may have on someone else. It can be hard to hear our own biases until someone helps us recognize them.

I think of my mom and my grandma. My mom contracted polio as a child, and it was a terrible experience physically and emotionally. People would walk away from her out of fear of contracting the virus themselves. I have compassion that this left scars on the whole family.

What I can't reconcile is that my Gramma continued to speak fear and shame over my mom for the rest of her life. Maybe she was never able to reconcile the fear of almost losing her child. But she allowed it to shadow their lives, and those fears gained a life of their own.

My mother didn't believe she could succeed or get the life she deserved. My Gramma was too afraid of the world caving in on her when she least expected it and couldn't step out of that fear. I learned not to trust, because they transferred their fear to me. And I readily accepted it, not knowing anything different.

Because of that shame, I saw "little" sins creep in and seem acceptable, which had devastating consequences. I learned how to lie early. It seemed like such a small thing. My mom would hide the bills from my dad so she could either pay them or talk about them with him on a day he wasn't tired from work. That doesn't seem harmful, assuming she's trying to protect his feelings.

But that wasn't it. She was trying to protect herself. She was still charging credit cards that she and my dad had paid off and cut up together, agreeing they wanted to stay out of debt. But she was still using credit behind his back and paying the bills without telling him what she'd done.

A little sin modeled at a crucial age. It set me up to believe that "small" lies were acceptable, especially with your spouse. I was telling myself it was a little lie that was protecting my husband, rather than acknowledging the truth: I was trying to protect myself from the ramifications of my sin. Another chink in the armor of my integrity. One I didn't even see myself.

But that "little" sin feels a little bigger when someone who also learned sin modeling hides extramarital relationships or their addiction to pornography from you. It suddenly doesn't feel small and protective. It feels like a big sin that they're intentionally hiding. Which is true in both cases. That little omission grew up into a pattern that repeated itself into something much bigger.

Where Our Beliefs Come From

After generational history, my counselor and I talked about my upbringing. We needed to evaluate what had impacted me and where my beliefs came from. Think about where your beliefs were formed in your own life. Some of our beliefs were formed by watching our parents. We saw how they interacted together, with other people, and with our siblings. Maybe they modeled faith for us, maybe they prioritized other values.

Did your family spend time together on the weekends doing fun activities? Did they teach you to love nature or various sports or animals? When did they start to teach you responsibility? How did you learn to interact with other kids and with other adults?

What did they teach you about your own self-worth? Did they teach you to believe in yourself? Did you feel safe to express emotions? Did anyone listen to your feelings?

We're also influenced by teachers and leaders in our lives, whether that's in school, our broader family, in our community, or in a church. Sometimes, looking back, it's hard to know where some of our beliefs came from.

There may be people or events we remember very clearly, especially if there was trauma involved. The moment when a belief changed for you may be seared in your mind. This is especially true if, in that moment, you stopped believing in someone, or a fantasy you believed was crushed. These moments are heartbreaking.

This is also where those who want to manipulate you and those who have traumatized you have undue influence over your character and your beliefs. It's easy to accept what a strong character in your life is telling you is the truth, especially if you've been molded to be even partially submissive to them.

When you look at your own life, evaluate where your beliefs originated. Look at who taught them to you. Were they a trustworthy teacher? Are they someone whose life you respect today? Did someone who had influence over you teach you wrong beliefs?

I ask these questions because I want you to start evaluating whether the belief you have is helpful or hurtful. Sorting out this difference can help you identify a belief's origin.

Where Our Beliefs Betrayed Us

Let's look at some examples from my story. I told you I grew up in a small conservative church, in an era where religion was often fear-based. This translated to a legalistic interpretation of the Bible. I believed you had to follow the rules or God would punish you, and love was only earned through my obedience and achievements, not freely given by grace.

I also believed human love was earned. I was praised when I performed perfectly, but if I was slightly less than perfect, my mom would voice her disappointment. I tried comparative analysis tactics with her, even at a young age, but that was met with the challenge of "you can do better."

What went wrong for me is that I interpreted this criticism as God's standard too. I believed I had to perform for God to love me.

In hindsight, I'm sure that belief was a combination of a legalistic church structure and the performance narrative I learned from a narcissistic parent.

These beliefs influenced my view of God's love. I didn't understand unconditional love, and I didn't know how to look for it. When I searched for a marriage partner, I took the first version of love I could find, because I was desperate to find love.

Not only was I trying to earn love, but I was also trying to earn my redemption. I tried success in all things to earn that reward—home, relationships, career, and service. None of that achieved my redemption, and my focus was so narrowed in on performing, I didn't have time to hear God's voice.

These misconceptions may sound familiar to you. Take a look at your own upbringing and the beliefs you were taught. It's okay to recognize that some of them need to change. We're here to do that together.

These beliefs led me to bad relationship choices. A scarcity mindset told me I needed to take love when it was offered because I wouldn't get another chance. A self-worth centered on success in marriage and family told me I was unworthy on my own. A performance narrative twisted these together to say I could earn my redemption by performing well in my relationships.

How do we stop ourselves from being deceived by a twisting of the truth? By knowing the truth because we've placed it in our hearts and recited it over and over so that we don't doubt it. If we're not sure we really know it, we won't know how to spot the lie. It will sound a lot like truth, and it will seem to make sense to us.

Recentering

Here's where I want to take a minute to center our thinking. So far it may sound like I'm blaming my relationship failures on a questionable upbringing. I'm not laying blame at my parents' feet or even my partners' feet. I made choices that influenced those outcomes. We were all contributors.

What I am saying is that my beliefs influenced the choices I made. Those beliefs were influenced by people, by circumstances, and choices others made before me. I say that with grace. We're all learning as we go, none of us has life figured out until we're in eternity.

I'm also not saying I deserved to be manipulated or emotionally abused. No one does. And if you're like me, let me pause and say I'm sorry. I'm sorry for what you experienced and what you've been through in dealing with the impact it had on your life. Life is hard and messy, and we all need loving support to survive it.

I do want you to consider if even some of your bad experiences are what drew you closer to God. Going through hard things likely increased your thirst for his truth, for a way to recenter your life into the right beliefs.

This is where we can make a difference in our lives and change the direction we're going. By learning the truth, by understanding right beliefs, and making choices out of both of those. How do we learn to do that? We first have to learn the truth to allow it to influence our lives.

God's Word is the source of truth in our lives. That's where we need to go to understand him and to understand ourselves. That longing we hold all our lives is only met by God, who is the one who can truly love us. We weren't meant to do life alone. We have the Holy Spirit in our lives to partner with us on this journey. As we move towards learning how to reframe our beliefs, I want you to first look back at what you learned about unconditional love.

Unconditional Love

Consider a time in your life when you could remember feeling free and unhindered, before the world clouded your beliefs. Look back at the peace and joy your heart knew; remember how you understood subconsciously to believe in yourself.

You could do great things; you knew nothing would get in your way. Becoming an astronaut, a firefighter, a sports hero, or a famous actress was a realistic goal for your life. What were you passionate about? What did you dream of? Hold that memory in mind because we're going to need it as a reference.

Growing up, I knew I was loved, but my parents didn't often say the words "I love you" until later in my life. The closest thing I can remember to feeling loved and fully supported was time with my dad—just the two of us. He'd let me ride with him on the old blue Ford tractor while he ploughed the ground for planting. We'd take hikes together and sometimes just sit under the trees and absorb their beauty.

We rarely spoke; words weren't needed. There were no expectations at that moment, being together was enough. It was a feeling of peace. My father was better at showing his support for me in actions than expressing his feelings in words.

My grandad was better able to express his love for me in words. He always took the time to tell me how beautiful, smart, and sweet I was. He'd write me notes on birthday cards and pick out the perfect gift he knew I'd enjoy. I was the apple of his eye, and he told me every chance he had. It was wonderful that he knew how to speak those words over me.

My dad would show his support in many ways over the years. He showed up for every FFA project and competition. He celebrated my awards along the way. He traveled across the country to celebrate my college graduation, even when that meant delaying his chemo treatments, because he knew how important it was to show me his heart.

Who was that person for you growing up? Your childhood memory of love and support may be outside the circle of your immediate family. Take a minute to picture them in your mind. Remember a scenario where they expressed to you how valuable you were.

- Take a few minutes to journal about this memory. Try to pull in everything your senses remember. What did that look like? Is there a particular scent that reminds you of this time? Is there a feeling of warmth or safety? Wrap yourself in that feeling of love and support.

- How would it feel to have that message played over you

in your life today? What does unconditional love and support look like to you as an adult? Is that message the same one you heard as a child, and you need to remember? Has that message expanded into something more today, based on where life has brought you now?

- Write down the messages you need to hear in your heart today.

- Pray over the message you heard as a child, and thank God for the support you were given. Now ask him to speak over you the words you need to hear today.

- Selah: Take some time to pause here and let those words wash over you throughout the day.

Can you think of a time when you believed God did not have your best interests in mind? Sometimes it can feel that way because we don't like our circumstances, or they don't make sense to us. But do we have any evidence against him? For me, it's always my choices that bring painful consequences.

Just like Thomas, who chose to doubt, I do too. But God is generous. He gave Thomas a second chance and answered his need to let go of his doubt. The second time, Thomas believed.

God gives us second chances as well. He hears our heart's cry for the reassurance we so desperately want from him. It's okay to be honest with him about our doubts and our unbelief. But we also need to be willing to admit when we're choosing to hang onto the hurt and doubt as our safety instead of trusting God.

Will you make that same choice in your own life? Will you choose to believe in the second chance God has offered you? If you will, then also believe in the better story he has for the future when you trust him with it.

But how do you know when he's giving you a second chance? When you're ready to step out and lead, how can you know which way he's taking you? Immersing ourselves in God's Word, so we know the truth, will teach us how to recognize his voice. Being a strong leader is one who knows and hears God's voice. Without that source of truth, our emotions and wandering thoughts can take us in the wrong direction. Let's learn how to do that by looking at God's Word together.

Chapter 3
Reframing Our Beliefs with Truth

Do you know the story in the Bible of laying out a fleece? If you didn't grow up with this story, let me give you the highlights. This is the story of Gideon, which we find in Judges 6 and 7. In Judges 6:14, God appoints Gideon to rescue the Israelites from the Midianites. Gideon questions God and asks how this will be possible. God tells him he would be with him (Jg 6:16). But still Gideon asks for a sign to confirm this is true. When Gideon brings an offering, an angel of the Lord accepts his offering.

Next God asks for Gideon's obedience to destroy the pagan altar of Baal. Gideon obeys. After he is obedient, God clothes him in power. But Gideon is still looking for confirmation from God.

In Judges 6:36-40, Gideon asks God to confirm for him that he heard what God said by showing him with a fleece he will leave out overnight. If the fleece is wet in the morning and the ground is dry, that would be his sign from God. God answers just as Gideon had requested.

Gideon still hesitates and asks God for the opposite sign the next night, meaning the fleece is dry and the ground is wet. God again did as he asked. After three confirmations, Gideon goes on to destroy the Midianites, as God has promised.

What do we learn from this story? First, Gideon knew God's voice and yet questioned God's words because they seemed impossible to him. I think we can end up in the same place. We may not know God well enough to recognize his voice, but even if we do, we struggle to believe he can change our lives.

Second, it's also worth noting that God is gracious enough to give Gideon three signs of confirmation. God understands our weaknesses. He knows our fears and disbeliefs, and he wants us to know him better and to trust him. He will continue to prove to us he is exactly who he says he is, and he'll do exactly what he says he'll do. We have to get to know him well enough to fully trust him.

To successfully lead others, we want to stay in tune with God's voice in our lives, so we lead in the direction he wants us to lead. But how do we recognize his voice if we don't know him very well? The more we can learn about God's character, about who he really is, the more his voice will naturally resonate in our hearts and mind.

Our Beliefs about God's Character

Evaluating our beliefs has led us to desire to know the truth. Drawing closer to God is the journey of our lives. His desire is for us to know him fully, to learn to trust him. Then we can walk in the path he created for us.

First, we've learned we need to know the truth and make decisions from a position of truth. Knowing God's character helps us easily identify his truth as we lead out. And one of the best places to learn that is in his Word.

Let's look first at an example of **God's character** together.

- Ps. 34:9-10, Ps. 37:4 – God is gracious to us and gives us good things.

The Truth: God is gracious to me and gives me good things.

What does your heart say to this truth? Listen to your feelings without trying to rationalize them or turn them into what you were taught to believe. Jot down your initial reactions. Are they positive or negative?

I respond negatively when I hear it. There's a part of my heart that says I don't deserve good things, I'm not worthy. This is the part of me that believes God doesn't see me; he wants good things for others, but not for me. He may occasionally give me good things, but he doesn't desire the best for me. When I dig deeper, I continue to hear the message of "second best."

I didn't see graciousness modeled to me as a child. I heard blame and ridicule if I didn't live up to my mom's expectations. I learned early how to put on a mask of happiness in all scenarios. If we embarrassed Mom, we would hear about it later.

It was later in life that gifts came with a price tag or an expectation. They always required an abundant acknowledgement of the giver. Any perceived lack of appreciation was reciprocated with admonition and guilt. My husband would berate me with defensive arguments, reminding me how much he'd given me if I dared to express any feelings of dissatisfaction with our relationship.

I don't deserve good things.

I don't understand graciousness.

Gifts were not something to look forward to because they came with attachments or expectations.

What did those beliefs lead to?

My disbelief in my own worth set me up to believe I didn't deserve good in my life. I would accept less than ideal, because I didn't expect to have anything better than that. That was most dramatically expressed in whom I accepted as a partner in my life. Rather than holding out for God's best for me, I was thrilled with attention from men who met the minimum criteria. I didn't believe I deserved more; I accepted the philosophy that this was as good as I could expect.

I had been swept off my feet with generous gifts at the start of my marriage. I equated gifts with love initially, until I became aware of the entanglements they brought with them. I became distrustful of gifts because I didn't like the expectations that came with them. That also meant I didn't trust the gift givers, which started with people but also translated to how I viewed God as well.

I didn't know how to be gracious with others or myself. I was quick to judge intent without first considering circumstances or motivation. I often assumed the worst, whether towards other people who had intended to be hurtful, or believing I must have done something wrong. I also didn't know how to forgive myself since I carried the blame for my mistakes and other people's feelings.

What does God's Word say about who he is?

Let's compare my beliefs against the truth in God's Word.

- *"Fear the Lord, you his godly people, for those who fear him will have all they need. Even strong young lions sometimes go hungry, but those who trust in the Lord will lack no good thing."* Ps. 34:9-10

- *"Take delight in the Lord, and he will give you your heart's desires."* Ps. 37:4

My heart loves these reminders that God wants to shower his children with good things and fulfill our hearts' desires. I can pause and let my heart be filled with his love for me. I don't have to keep grasping at what the world has offered. But it comes first with a heart that's seeking God.

Fear the Lord, seek the Lord, delight yourself in the Lord. Those are the words God leads with in these passages. We must have our perspective in the right place before he will give us the desires of our hearts. He won't give us anything we could possibly wish for; He'll give us the desires of our hearts when our hearts are focused on him.

Our new beliefs redefined through God's truth:

My Father loves me with an unconditional love. He always wants the best for my life. His desire is to give me good things.

Let's look another example together:

- Ps. 9:10 - God can be trusted, he does not abandon us.

The Truth: God can be trusted. He does not abandon us.

This was a tough one to believe for a long time. Most people in my life had proved they were untrustworthy and abandoned me. I believed God would do the same. Maybe this is similar for you. Have you struggled to trust people in your life because you've been hurt? Have you felt abandoned by parents, siblings, co-workers, friends, or others? We can put up stubborn defenses.

Do you trust others?
Do you trust God?
Do you believe God will not abandon you?

What do those beliefs lead to?

Because I believed God to be untrustworthy, I thought I could only rely on myself. You may have had the same response. Are you like me, stubbornly proving to the world you can do it yourself instead of asking for help when you need it?

Do you assume people will leave you, so you push them away before they leave you? I still work against my fight-or-flight responses in some scenarios. At the first sign of something I'm afraid of trusting in a relationship, I want to leave rather than ask questions or work through the issue.

What does God's Word say?

- *"Those who know your name trust in you, for you, O Lord, do not abandon those who search for you."* Ps. 9:10

- *"Do not be afraid or discouraged, for the Lord will personally go ahead of you. He will be with you; he will neither fail you nor abandon you."* Dt. 31:8

These verses also require our action. We need to trust in God, we need to search for him. We are not to give into fear or discouragement. We need to know who God is so we can trust him. That's true in any relationship. We get to know someone, so we know their character. We can know who God is the more we spend time in his Word.

It also tells us to search for him. We need to seek him. God doesn't want us to only call on him in our moments of desperation, then ignore him the rest of the time. We need to seek a relationship with him like we would any good friend.

We also have to remind ourselves who God is, how he's different from other relationships in our lives. He promises he won't abandon us, and we can trust him to be true to his Word. He won't fail us. You get to choose to believe him and his Word. You can choose to believe what his Word says about him as truth.

Our new beliefs redefined through God's truth:

God can be trusted because I know his character. He will never abandon me because he loves me.

Here are some more examples of God's character. Take some time to read these verses and hear God's truth spoken over you. Get to know him. Pick the ones you need to be reminded of the most, write them out, and put them where you will see them every day. Recite them over yourself daily. Memorize them. Hide them in your heart, so you will know the truth of who God is.

- Ps. 145:9, La. 3:22-23 – God cares about us.

- Ps. 34:7, Ps. 91:4, Ps. 121:3-4 – God is protecting us all the time.

- Ps. 9:10, Is. 26:4 – God can be trusted.

- Je. 9:24, Ho.11:3-4 – God is kind.

- Nu. 23:19, He. 6:18 – God never lies.

- Nu. 23:19, Ps. 145:13 – God follows through on all his promises.

- Ps. 100:3, Is. 64:8, Ma. 2:10 – God made us; therefore, he knows what's best for us.

- Dt. 7:9, Ps. 33:4 – God's faithfulness will never let us down.

- I Jn. 3:1, I Jn. 4:9 – God has a passionate love for us.

- Dt. 32:4, Ps. 145:17 – God's heart is absolutely pure.

- Dt. 7:9, Je. 31:3 – God's love for us is without limit.

- Ps. 100:5, Na. 1:7 – God is good.

Selah.

Personal Beliefs – Your Identity in Christ

It's also important to know how God sees us. We get such a mixed-up view of ourselves based on the inputs we get from the world. I was trying to be a good person and live the Christian life, but not doing it from a heart that truly understood God and how he saw me.

I thought if I did the right things, my heart would fall in line. But it didn't work that way. I was doing the service, but my heart was still broken. I was still trying to earn my redemption.

There were moments I heard his voice and worked on changing my beliefs. I was trying to set the truth of how he sees me in my heart, but I was so early in the process. I hadn't given myself the time to heal or to really hear his words over me. I wasn't consistently seeking him and hearing his voice, so I let the voices of those around me overpower his truth.

I didn't spend enough time with him to know him at a deep heart level. It left a big hole in my heart I was trying to fill. I didn't know who I was. I believed I wasn't whole alone. I found my identity in serving other people, and only by their appreciation could I have any worth.

I hadn't let the truth of God's Word permeate my life. I read the words of how he sees me, but I kept my heart closed. Those were great words, but only true for those who hadn't sinned. Or who was stronger in their faith. Yes, God loved me, but I was at the back of the line.

I'd get into heaven; I had given my life to him. But I wasn't getting rewarded, he didn't look forward to my arrival, and I wouldn't be welcomed with open arms. I wasn't going to be wrapped in the loving embrace of someone who missed me and was overjoyed to see me.

That was for the perfect ones, and I was far from that. My sins were unforgivable. I was the forgotten stepdaughter, no one really missed or asked about.

I didn't understand that God's love is different than human love. I still don't fully understand it, but I'm learning. I'm leaning into him. I'm refusing to accept anything less. Let's look at what he tells us about our identity.

Our Identity in Christ:

- Ro. 8:32-39 – God truly loves me.

Now let's take this verse and look at our hearts and God's Word.

The Truth: God truly loves me.

Close your eyes for a minute, read that truth again, and listen to your initial reactions.

What do I hear when I hear those words? My head says yes, I know that to be true, his Word says so, and I believe his Word is truth. But my heart says yes, that's true for everyone else, except for me, because I'm not lovable. I don't have it together, I'm not perfect. I'm not as good as people think. I'm not pure. I'm unworthy as a woman because I'm not a mother in the way the world expects it. No one wants to know the real me. I don't deserve to be loved, I'm not worthy.

My sin gets in the way. I've repented of what I've done wrong, and I've asked God's forgiveness. But is it enough? My heart feels like I've made too many bad choices, and I've reached the quota for sin. At times I knew better, but I still made bad choices. Some of the things I've done are unforgivable.

Here's where I got lost, maybe you're there with me. I was comparing God's love to human love. I didn't really understand God's love, so I looked at what I've seen in my life. In my growing up years, I had one distant parent and one parent who didn't know how to love me. But I desperately tried to earn their love anyway. I would receive accolades for perfect work, for winning competitions; that seemed to make them happy. I didn't understand that wasn't love. They didn't know how to give love; I assumed I had done something wrong because they weren't expressing their love towards me. I didn't comprehend unconditional love.

I'm not worthy of love.

My sins are unforgivable.

What do those beliefs lead to?

I became very performance-oriented. I felt I had to earn love by pleasing other people. Because my sins were unforgivable, I could never work hard enough or do enough for others to earn their love. It was a never-ending cycle. I desperately wanted to get better, to do better, to somehow get ahead on this treadmill I had created for myself. But it was impossible on my own.

I thought rescuing others would somehow earn me my redemption. That was an overwhelming undertaking. Honestly impossible. I was the one who needed rescuing. Even if they did too, I was the only person I could change. That's hard to accept.

What does God's Word say?

Ro. 8:32-39

> *32 Since he did not spare even his own Son but gave him up for us all, won't he also give us everything else? 33 Who dares accuse us whom God has chosen for his own? No one—for God himself has given us right standing with himself. 34 Who then will condemn us? No one—for Christ Jesus died for us and was raised to life for us, and he is sitting in the place of honor at God's right hand, pleading for us.*
>
> *35 Can anything ever separate us from Christ's love? Does it mean he no longer loves us if we have trouble or calamity, or are persecuted, or hungry, or destitute,*

or in danger, or threatened with death? ³⁶ *(As the Scriptures say, "For your sake we are killed every day; we are being slaughtered like sheep.")* ³⁷ *No, despite all these things, overwhelming victory is ours through Christ, who loved us.*

³⁸ *And I am convinced that nothing can ever separate us from God's love. Neither death nor life, neither angels nor demons, neither our fears for today nor our worries about tomorrow—not even the powers of hell can separate us from God's love.* ³⁹ *No power in the sky above or in the earth below—indeed, nothing in all creation will ever be able to separate us from the love of God that is revealed in Christ Jesus our Lord.*

My trouble was that I stayed in my limiting beliefs. I chose to believe I wasn't good enough. I didn't want to acknowledge my sins; I wasn't willing to forgive myself. It didn't matter that God had forgiven me, I thought I knew better. I thought I deserved more punishment than I had already felt, that was the only way to my redemption.

But you see, that's not the way God works. He won't continue to punish us. He doesn't see us as failures who will never change. My failed experiences trying to convince people with addictions to change colored my view of myself. I lost confidence in *my* ability to change, so I stopped believing I had the strength in me to change. Once a sinner, always a sinner, or so I thought.

But that's not God's view of us. He doesn't even include the "once a sinner" part in the description, even though he could. He could say, "once a sinner, but now redeemed." That could be the right view for us to keep perspective on how much he's done for us. But honestly, he says our sins are as far as the east is from the west. He's put them out of his mind, out of his sight completely. His description of us is *my beloved child, pure and blameless in my sight*. Sin is not mentioned, our past is not mentioned, he doesn't think of it at all.

If God is not accusing us, why are we accusing ourselves? His Word says NO ONE but him can accuse us. NO ONE can condemn us. That includes us, my sisters. We can't accuse and condemn ourselves. Only God can. And he chooses not to. He chooses to forgive and truly forget.

I'm still learning to mirror that kind of forgiveness to others in my life. Some days I keep a record of wrongs. I'll forgive, but with hesitation. I'm not ready to trust you because you've wronged me before. In the same way, I don't always believe in myself because I've messed up before.

This is still a struggle for me because I've been hurt by people who would use that kind of forgiveness against me to keep sinning, to keep taking advantage. Maybe that's true for you as well. I have to hand them over to the Lord. My accusing them isn't helping anything. It's only making me miserable. Let God deal with their sins; my responsibility is for my own heart, and my relationship with the Lord. Boundaries with people are healthy, all of us are a work in progress.

Redefining our beliefs through God's truth:

I get to remind myself every day that God truly loves me—with an amazing love that I don't understand and didn't earn. I can speak those words over myself every minute that doubt creeps in during the day. I can set aside my old beliefs. Awareness helps here too. When I hear myself speaking untruth in how I talk to myself, I have to catch the words and stop them, then replace them with truth. I have to stop looking for approval in others or trying to redeem myself. Only God's love for me and his gift of salvation will redeem me.

I get to accept God's unconditional love for me. I don't need another person to do this for me. I am completely fulfilled by my heavenly Father. I am confident in his love for me. I say his words over my life every day, so that my mind and heart will start to align with his truths. He loves me more than anyone has ever loved me.

I am repentant when I sin, I set my sins at his feet, and I can accept God's forgiveness. I don't get to continue to accuse and condemn myself for my mistakes. I lay down my words of condemnation and pick up his words of love.

Turning our new identities into strengths:

Once I accept God's love and learn to love myself, I get better at loving those around me. I can be more compassionate to my family and friends because I can understand when they struggle and make mistakes like I do. I can forgive them, just like I can forgive myself.

If this is a struggle for you, I encourage you to spend some time reading these additional verses about our identity in Christ.

Our Identity in Christ:

- Ro. 8:32-39, Ep. 3:17-19, 1 Jn. 4:10, 4:16 – God truly loves me.

- Mt. 3:17 – God dearly loves us, and we bring him great joy.

- Dt. 7:9, Ps. 89:24, 2 Th. 3:3 – It is God's desire to be faithful to me.

- 2 Co. 6:19-20, Ep. 1:5, 2:6 – I am important to God.

- Is. 57:15-18, Ez. 36:24-30 – I am not a bad person, even though I have done bad things.

- Jn. 1:12, Ro. 8:15-17 – God believes I am worth embracing as his child.

- Ps. 103:3, 1 Jn. 1:9 – There is no sin I have committed that God won't forgive.

- 2 Sa. 11:14-17, Ac. 13:22 – Even though I may have experienced or done horrible things, it doesn't define who I am.

- Jn. 15:15-16, 1 Jn. 5:14 – I can ask God for what I want and need.

- Is. 61:1, Je. 33:6, Ho. 11:3-4 – God considers my life

worth healing.

- Ps. 139:14, Ec. 3:11 – I am a valuable person and worth getting to know.

Do any of these verses stick out to you? Make you happy or angry? Examine your feelings and beliefs about your identity. Is your view of yourself aligned with how God sees you? Or have you allowed the world to color your view? Take some time to recenter your beliefs with his truth.

Continue this process with another daily activity: speak these words over your life. Let them sink into your memory and resound in your mind. If possible, find them in a song so they will permanently embed themselves in your mental archives.

It's the first step to start actually living with these reframed beliefs. And the first steps to being able to teach and lead others. Our own hearts need to know the truth at our deepest levels for us to be the authentic leaders people want to follow. Take the time to change your heart and mind.

Chapter 4
Learning to Live in Truth

Once I started reframing my beliefs, I realized I needed to change my life as well. Suddenly, I could see where my choices weren't aligned with what I truly believed. They were aligned with my old beliefs, and I didn't want to be that person anymore. I had been listening to other people's beliefs, as well as the negative self-talk track in my own mind.

If I wanted to start making wiser choices, I had to start catching myself in the act of talking negatively and start speaking differently to myself.

Our words are much more powerful than we realize.

What we tell ourselves is what we come to believe about ourselves. I had been reinforcing the wrong beliefs in my own mind long enough that I didn't even realize that I was doing it. The message of God's judgement was much stronger than the message of his love.

If we want to change our limiting beliefs, we have to change what we speak over ourselves, as well as what we allow others to speak over us. For me it came in stages. I had to stop beating myself up, because I wasn't believing in who I could be. I certainly didn't believe in who God made me to be.

I started to catch myself muttering that I was an idiot under my breath. But I could no longer speak that over myself once I believed that I was a child of God, made in his image. I had to keep listening and hearing where I had allowed the wrong words into my mind and replace them with the affirmations that I knew to be true from Scripture. Even still, I have to remind myself who I am and who I want to be.

Now that I had changed that belief to understand how much God loves me and how he was gracious to me, I could no longer hold my past mistakes over my head in condemnation. Once I believed God wanted the best for my life, I had to believe he would bring good things to me once I leaned into him in prayer and turned towards his desires.

I was starting to hear God's love throughout my life. I was evaluating my life to become better aligned with what I truly believed and what I wanted to see. But I needed to get better at hearing the truth in the world around me. That was going to take more learning and more practice.

Discernment

Discernment gives us the ability to separate truth from untruth and to measure against the source of truth. The first time I tried to segregate between what was true and what was fiction in the stories I was being told was with a good counselor. He taught me to segregate black versus white in the scenarios I lived through. Many times, I had believed a story to be true because I knew part of it was true. The many years of listening to a manipulator and being gaslit had turned all things into shades of gray.

My ex-husband was an expert at taking a small piece of the truth and weaving it into his story. That small piece of truth made me doubt what I knew. It made me think I could believe the whole story. He would leverage that small truth against me and guilt me into believing everything he was saying. What I didn't realize is that I was accepting his story without evaluating it for truth, and he had proved himself untrustworthy.

I had to get better at evaluating his story against the full truth. But it took a while to be able to clear out all the gray he had clouded my thoughts with to see black and white again. Once I could challenge him on the partial truth, my vision and my understanding began to clear.

That turns out to be true across many areas of our lives. We might experience this at work when someone is trying to persuade you to their interpretation of an event or to guilt you into doing their work for them. We might see this in our friendships if they are hiding the truth from us. We might see it in our families, in our closest relationships. How do we learn to discern the truth?

First, we have to know the truth. We have to know God's Word well enough to recognize when we're hearing something different. When we've filled our minds with the truth, then the lies won't sound right, won't ring true with what we've learned.

To do this means we have to choose to be in God's Word daily. It helps to be in a Bible study with other believers so you can learn from them as well. It's also key to start memorizing Scripture so it stays in our memory and permeates our minds.

Second, we have to learn to listen to the Holy Spirit, to allow his voice to speak over our lives, and to make the Word of God clear to us. This can sound nebulous. How do we do this?

I think the key is taking the time to listen. For me that's usually in the quiet spaces—taking a walk, going on a hike, sitting in the yard listening to the birds, or just pausing in a quiet evening to take in the silence. My soul must still before I can listen.

Sometimes this also looks like working on routine tasks that don't take mental investment, like doing dishes or cleaning and organizing a room. Sometimes my heart is so spun up, I have to keep my hands busy to get my mind to relax.

Either way, the key is to be open to listening. I know it can be hard to shut off our busy lives and the many lists swirling in our heads to truly listen. But giving ourselves the quiet space to listen can become part of our routine. Start with a few minutes and work up to longer times where you settle into your quiet space and listen for God's leading.

As believers, we now have the mind of Christ. Because we are filled with the Holy Spirit, we can understand God's Word and hear his leading. I know for me, trying to understand Scripture can feel overwhelming at times. I don't feel equipped.

Paul tells us in 1 Co. 2:10-12, *"But it was to us that God revealed these things by his Spirit. For his Spirit searches out everything and shows us God's deep secrets. No one can know a person's thoughts except that person's own spirit, and no one can know God's thoughts except God's own Spirit. And we have received God's Spirit (not the world's spirit), so we can know the wonderful things God has freely given us."*

Paul reminds us that we can now interpret Scriptures and understand them because the Holy Spirit dwells within us and can give us all insight. God gives us his insight within us to draw upon any time we ask. That's a resource we can all use!

Also note, this verse tells us the Holy Spirit searches out everything. God is working to reveal to us those areas of doubt in our hearts and helping us to understand his heart for us. He will show us the truth he wants us to understand, if we're open to listening and hearing his voice.

Ph. 1:9-11: *"And this is my prayer: that your love may abound more and more in knowledge and depth of insight, so that you may be able to discern what is best and may be pure and blameless for the day of Christ, filled with the fruit of righteousness that comes through Jesus Christ—to the glory and praise of God"* (NIV).

Here, Paul is reminding us in his prayer that that's what he wants for us—that we grow in knowledge and depth of insight. That's what we need to draw on for our discernment to grow—time in God's Word and listening to the Holy Spirit. Not only will these actions increase our discernment, but they will help us live those truths out in our lives. Those actions will have repercussions in our lives. We will become more pure, blameless, and filled with God's righteousness.

Let's look at how we can apply this. Let's go back to the snake in the garden of Eden. The words Satan used were not "God doesn't trust you with the whole truth, he wants to keep things hidden from you." No, that would have been too obvious. It was just a question: "Can't you eat from any tree in the garden?"

Note the subtle difference. One statement boldly argues with the truth, and Eve would have recognized that for the lie it was. Instead, it's a small hint that leads Eve to question her own beliefs without Satan having to directly confront her on them. He plants a seed of doubt and lets her own mind do the rest.

It's the same tactics he's still using on us today. And the same tactics our abusers used against us. It may be the first documented evidence of manipulation and gaslighting, before we knew there were words for it. "Surely God wants you to enjoy all the fruit of the garden," which is code for "Why would God limit you?" God had Eve's best interests in mind and was asking her to be obedient to him and to have faith in his plan.

It's the same that he's asking of us today. He is asking for our obedience, and for us to trust him, to have faith in his plan for our lives. By working to increase our discernment, we listen for God's voice speaking in our lives. As we lean into his voice and his plan, we can let go of our doubt and mistrust. That's where we can strengthen our faith.

I would also note here that we need to stay vigilant against sin in our lives. Unconfessed sin can limit our ability to hear the Holy Spirit's prompting. Keep listening to where God is asking you for increased purity, and continue to turn those areas over to him.

Trusting Your Intuition

Now let's look at discernment from a different angle. We've been discussing discernment from the spiritual side, but let's also consider being discerning with ourselves. For many of us who have been through trauma, we've learned to ignore our body's reactions to our situations so we could survive them. But now that we're in a safe place, we've also got to learn to listen to our intuition. One of the best ways to do that is to pay attention to our physical reactions that happen before our brains can process the situation.

In my case, the many years of gaslighting had convinced me I couldn't trust my own intuition. I had to learn to listen to my own reactions, trust that flutter in my heart, or the nausea that came up when I thought about an event or seeing someone. I had to learn to feel my feelings rather than disconnect my physical reactions from my emotional state.

My feelings were hard to recognize at first. I had stuffed them or ignored them for so long that I didn't recognize them. I had to sit with myself and my reactions to know what I was feeling and to try to understand why. I had to have enough compassion for myself to allow whatever emotions came up, and enough strength to know the emotions themselves couldn't overrule me.

This is another area that takes some time to understand and develop—and sometimes with the help of a good counselor. But it's okay to stop stuffing your emotions and let your body tell you what it's feeling. Sometimes your fight or flight reaction is for good reason, and you should listen to that. Sometimes its old memories replaying over your current situation, and you have to allow yourself to let go of those emotions, forgive the original scenario, and find a new way to step forward.

Your body will likely need to heal in a myriad of ways that you don't expect. Stored trauma can wreak havoc on you physically, not just on your emotions. Take the time to share what you're feeling with a professional and get the help you need to heal.

Once you can start to recognize what you're feeling, you can name that emotion and find the source of that emotion. Then, in the same way we process forgiveness, we can let go of that emotion. We can forgive ourselves for feeling this way, we can lay it at God's feet, and we can allow him to fill us with a new emotion and a new reaction. We can take the time to pause, assess our emotions, and discern if they are appropriate before we react.

I do believe our intuition is often Spirit-led. It's a different way to hear God's voice. Our subconscious mind can read someone's actions, and our body can tell us before our brain knows how to put it into words. That's where we need to allow credence to our emotions but then check in with the Holy Spirit. It's okay to ask whether our reaction is coming from the Holy Spirit or from our own history of trauma.

By growing our discernment, it gives us the keys to start living in a way that is true to ourselves—true to our beliefs, true to our identity, and living out of a healed state. But it can also help us to be more discerning of the people around us, who we allow in our circle of trust, and how we can minister to others.

The more in tune we are with the Holy Spirit, the more we'll be able to recognize what our emotions are telling us. He can give us insight into what others need and how we can help them. He can give insight into how we should pray for others, as well as specific ways we can help them.

At the same time, he will protect us, and we can trust him for that. He will give us insight into the people around us, for when we should trust them. If your body is telling you it feels unsafe around someone, listen to that reaction and ask yourself why you feel that way. Is there a subtle sign you recognize from previous history? Is there something in their character that makes you hesitate around them?

You can take that to the Holy Spirit and allow him to speak over you with wisdom. We may not always understand why at the time, but we can trust him to lead us. He'll tell us who we can fully trust and who we need to keep at arm's length.

This is such a gift for leadership and working with people. Our intuition can tell us where to trust people and where to hold back. It can help us see if someone's intentions are not pure. It can help us discern who is aligned with our teams' goals and culture and who wouldn't be a good fit. It can lead us in what people need to hear when we're ministering to them.

Authenticity: Aligning Our Beliefs with Our Actions

The challenge for me becomes taking this new identity into my everyday life. I pray to release my false beliefs and ask God to fill me with his view of me. But it can be so very easy to forget the next morning. I can pick up my spirit of fear and doubt in a heartbeat when I'm challenged with a new issue or situation. I have to remember to pray and to recenter my beliefs on the truth I know from God's Word and ask for his guidance for my day.

It's taken me time to learn how to be authentic with people. It felt like a constant hand slap as I tried to show people the real me. I'd been taught since I was little that people wouldn't like me unless I was perfect and had it together, looking good on the outside and presenting the "on-top-of-it" attitude. I was sure no one would want to see the messy feelings, at least not until I've had some time to process, sort, and organize them.

Dirt washes off easily, but those messy feelings turn into stains that feel like they'll never wash out, and everyone will start to notice them on me. That's how we carry much of our shame—in clothes that are yellowed with stains, never able to be clean and new and fresh again. That's why God reminds us we are "white as snow" when he forgives our sins (Is. 1:18).

The old me would remind myself and continue to condemn myself when I sin. I would forget to believe I'm redeemable, forget to see that God chooses to make me whole again. It can be hard to step forward in faith, especially when we've been taught to hesitate. With my reframed beliefs, I can allow myself grace and learn to trust again.

In our striving to make God relatable—someone we can talk to and reach out to—we can almost make him too human. In turn, we forget his power and majesty, that he is the one we can rely on to truly change our lives and transform us into the people he designed us to be. We have to see him as both the Father we can run to for comfort and understanding, as well as the God who saves us and has the power to change us.

I'm finding it gets easier to be authentic each time I step out in faith. We're all a bit messy, but people don't stop loving us because of it. It makes us who we are. Our story is what shapes us into who we are today. I want people to know me for who I am, and I want to continue to grow and learn.

We've all made bad choices along the way. The point is what choices we're making now. Who are we striving to be? It's okay to struggle on the journey. Sharing that struggle with those around us can help us through the process. Someone else will have a perspective you haven't thought of yet, which can help you as well.

The more we learn to accept ourselves, the less we worry about what others might think of us. The more we accept ourselves, the more we can accept others for exactly who they are as well. We can give each other grace. This allows us to live with more vulnerability than we've allowed in our lives for a long time.

Sharing our lives and our struggles can speak life into someone else's world. That moment of honesty helps them see you living as your authentic self, and people love that. We all want to be seen and loved for our true selves.

I will also note, you can live in authenticity without feeling like you have to confess your life story to everyone you know. You can be honest with things that you've been through and explain your struggles with authenticity, but ultimately, only your Heavenly Father knows every detail of your life and heart.

He is trustworthy with your whole story. He has already forgiven you for every choice you've made if you've asked him to. From there forward, you get to choose what you share based on how the Holy Spirit leads you. Lean into him to know how much to share, and don't be afraid to be vulnerable with people. Your past no longer gets to hurt you.

At that same time, being true to ourselves and being willing to be vulnerable will help others want to follow us as leaders. I believe in someone's expertise if they've done the work. We know this to be true in our work environment, but we can forget to translate that to our daily lives. We trust and respect the people around us who have found their way through hard things in life and come out stronger, and who aren't afraid to share that with people around them.

That's the kind of leader we want to be as well. Someone who's lived through the hard things and comes out stronger. A person who's taken the time to examine their beliefs against truth, until they understand them. And someone who is willing to honestly share their life and learnings to help enrich the lives of those around them. These are the leaders I respect the most, whom I want to align with and support.

Utilizing our discernment and intuition can help us to trust our reactions as truth. When we know the truth we can live authentically. Authenticity is just the beginning. It creates the foundation for healthy leadership. When we learn to live in the truth, we can extend that inward compassion to others and set the stage to become the type of leaders we all want to become.

Chapter 5
Giving Compassion

Yesterday was a day I needed compassion. I wasn't even in tune enough with my own feelings to realize it. I got the news that my neighbor next door to my parents' farm was diagnosed with cancer. Having moved away, I didn't get the news when it happened, so I was alone in my loss. My neighbor had been the mom everyone needs—she'd take time for coffee with you and help you with farm chores. She'd call and ask to meet at the fence so she could hand you a warm pie.

What I didn't realize was how I was feeling. I was there to check on the property, the portion of my parents' farm I still owned. Thankfully these neighbors had also cared for my property once I moved away. I had a couple friends with me to assess the trees. I felt busy with them, so I did my normal response and pushed down my emotions until I had time to process them. But I was too tired later that day to acknowledge how I was feeling.

The next day, I still didn't have time to think about my grief. I told my brother about it when I got home, and he said three different times how sorry he was. I was far more connected to my neighbors than my brother was, so he was right to assume it would impact me more than it did him.

My heart was silently hurting. When my brother expressed how sorry he was, it started to register that I was suppressing painful emotions. But it took a colleague expressing her sympathy as well for me to take a breath and acknowledge it. Later in the day, when I had a completely emotional response to a work issue, I realized I needed to take some time away for myself.

What I needed in that moment was compassion and understanding, and I wasn't looking for it anywhere I should have expected it. Work wasn't somewhere I would reach out to people for understanding. I needed to reach out to my personal network for that support, take the time to acknowledge and honor my feelings, and give myself the self-care and compassion I needed.

So I did. I took a nap, hopped into a warm shower, and went over to see some friends for a birthday party. I didn't share my news; I didn't need to. I just needed to be in the presence of friends for a while. Then I went shopping for a pile of ingredients to try some new recipes because the kitchen is always where I can process emotions.

What Compassion Looks Like

What is compassion? Concern for the sufferings or misfortunes of others. Compassion is the act or capacity for sharing the painful feelings of another with a desire to alleviate it. It's a feeling of kindness and care for another, to "suffer with." That's a perfect picture. When did Jesus suffer with me? When did I suffer with others?

The most vivid example of suffering with someone I can remember is when I sat with my grandmother when she lost her oldest daughter. My mom was out of town on a trip when the news came about her sister Betty. I went to spend time with Gramma.

I know she was doing her best to keep it together since I was the grandchild, and she didn't feel like she should break down in front of me. But she did cry some and we did a lot of sitting together, sometimes talking, sometimes not, just being together. I'd make tea when we needed it.

She talked to a few people on the phone. I couldn't do a lot. I couldn't change what had happened, but I could show her I loved her, and I was there for her. I could do the little things to help make her day easier.

Sometimes we can give compassion when we're able and feel called to do so. We can offer financial support to those who are suffering in other parts of the world. We can help build a house that someone can purchase at a lower price because of donated time and materials.

We can help a stranger in a moment of need. We can pay for a meal for someone we don't know. Or, open our homes and invite people in, become friends with those who are lonely.

Giving Compassion in the Wrong Places

There were many times in life when I wanted compassion and understanding from those around me. Sometimes, I didn't deserve it, and sometimes, I had to bear circumstances caused by the actions of people I loved.

When my first husband made bad decisions, I would try to help him deal with the consequences of his choices. In some areas, I gave him grace and support. It made sense after his surgery that I took on more of the chores around the house. I made sure he had healthy meals and could rest and recover. That kind of compassion is helpful and right.

What I didn't realize is that it's also easy to twist compassion and use it take advantage of those who are giving. When my husband started to take advantage of my compassion and used that to manipulate me, I started making unhealthy choices as well.

I would allow his use of the painkillers, thinking that's what most people need initially after surgery to help them rest and let their body recuperate. I believed him when he said using the medication was temporary, and he wouldn't get addicted to it again. I didn't know enough about addictions to understand that it wasn't the truth. He was already addicted again when he was telling me that.

But I furiously supported him because he was my husband, he was a good guy at heart, and I believed he wouldn't intentionally hurt me. I didn't know that an addict is like having a second person living inside of the person you love, someone very different from their original character. They look and sound like the person you love, but their motivations are very different.

My support for his bad choices was compassion he didn't deserve. At the time, I didn't understand why people weren't more compassionate towards me in the scenario. In my mind, they should have known that I was really trying to support him the best I knew how, and they should have given me grace in that.

In hindsight, I realize they were right to be less forthcoming with their compassion and question my motives in giving him as much grace as I did. I see now that my worth was tied up in his love for me, and I believed he would only keep loving me if I kept him happy. What I mistook for compassion was my feeble attempt at earning his love.

Giving Compassion

The first lesson of compassion we learn is how badly we need it for ourselves. We want others to show us grace and understanding. How many times did I want the world to give me a break, to show me some grace, to for once let me off the hook on even a small thing? And how often it felt like that would never come.

When I saw that other people needed compassion as much as I did was when I started to heal. Not just to those who were impacted by circumstances out of their control, we can all have compassion for that. Not just those who were hurting because of a medical issue, but also those who were hurting due to their bad choices.

We can have compassion for someone without condoning their behavior. We can choose to help someone who's made poor choices without letting them continue in their bad behavior. We can help and maintain healthy boundaries at the same time.

What I need most, and what we all need most, is God's compassion in our lives. I need to know I have a Savior who can give me grace even though I've made bad choices. Even though I've caused consequences that have made him sad. Even though I've hurt other people. I don't normally mean to hurt others, but sometimes my choices create unforeseen impacts.

That's when we need the most compassion from others—when we don't deserve it. When we've messed things up or hurt someone for selfish reasons. We don't deserve forgiveness or compassion. But God still freely gives us compassion. The people we hurt may not be able to give that compassion as easily as God can.

Losing Compassion

I've watched people struggle with addictions. I've lived beside them and watched them make terrible decisions with no thought of the long-term consequences. Their only thought in that moment is the next drink or the next high.

I don't want to believe I could fall prey to addictions and lose everything. The trouble is, I'm not safe from that possibility if I don't keep my heart focused on God. Addictive tendencies run in my family genes. Any of us, even without genetic influence, can hit a point where we're overwhelmed and masking the pain and anything sounds better than facing it.

I've also seen times in my life where I've given in to addictions and let them control my life. I made bad decisions as well. I didn't end up homeless and without a job, but I was living on the edge of ruin financially, and I made choices I regretted. Choosing to marry men with addictions contributed to the fact that I don't have children of my own today. I wish I'd made a better choice.

But God is good in all things. He's creating other opportunities for me that I might not have had time for if I were raising a family. Or maybe it's because I'm alone and can't focus my attention on someone else, he's able to get my attention and turn me to the healing I needed so desperately.

It took some time for me to realize how desperate my need was. How close to the edge of disaster I was on my own. I always wanted to convince myself I had things under control. How disillusioned I was.

I was trying to keep all the plates spinning in my life, mostly on my own, occasionally leaning into God for help. I think in hindsight, I was mostly trying to succeed in my own strength rather than truly leaning in and trusting God. Yet I believed I was a believer. I didn't know I wasn't really living faith out in my life.

I think that's how Satan tricks us. He encourages us to live life with sunglasses when it rains. We can see, but it's hazy. We go to church, we pray sometimes, and we occasionally read the Bible. But we don't give our hearts over to God. We feel his presence in the few moments we allow him in. We believe that's as good as it gets. We believe that about all of our life—this is as good as it gets, this is the most we can expect.

We convince ourselves to be grateful and content with mediocre, because we don't believe God will do more. We utilize him as our "get-out-of-jail-free" card that we hang onto until the end of the game. But we don't live our lives under the belief that he has already freed us from prison, and we can walk freely today.

We sit inside our prison walls, even though the door is open. We're too scared to face what's outside the walls. We don't believe our God is big enough to handle our doubts and fears.

You and I were beaten back so many times before when we tried to stretch our wings. We went through the motions, believing this was the most God had to offer—showing up for church, hearing the lesson, but not taking it into our hearts. Doing the "right" things on the checklist, instead of seeking the relationship with him that he desired for us.

When we give him all of our heart and trust him with our weaknesses is when we can truly give him our lives. We must admit how weak we are on our own.

For me, I had to turn my focus to God first. I had to learn to love myself again. I had to learn to see myself through God's eyes, wholly complete, fully loved, perfect and accepted just as I am. To realize that any time I felt alone or like no one loved me, I had the perfect companion, the perfect husband, the perfect friend in Jesus. I had to work on my relationship with him, take the time and make it a priority.

I had to learn to trust him. Most of this leadership journey is really about me learning. Learning to hear where I need to reframe my thinking. Learning where I need to love others more and see their lives through their lived experiences. That's where compassion comes from.

Giving Ourselves Compassion

Maybe even harder than accepting God's grace is being willing to give it to ourselves. We want to continue to beat ourselves up for our bad behavior rather than learning to accept ourselves as fallible. We don't want to need compassion. We want to be stronger than that. In a mixed-up way, we feel better when we punish ourselves, even when we really want to accept compassion. It's part of learning how to forgive ourselves as well.

This response was a lesson that had taken some time to learn. I had to learn how to give myself compassion. I was better at serving others, being empathetic to their needs.

I feel emotions strongly and I can empathize to the point of physically feeling someone else's pain. I do want to help others. I want to see them feel better physically, emotionally, and mentally. But I was also raised by a narcissist, so I'm trained to respond to and care for others more than I will care for myself.

I had to learn to give myself the grace I needed. I had to learn to take care of my needs. It's okay to need time off. It's okay to set boundaries with other people that allow you time to reset yourself emotionally. Self-care is not a gift we rarely deserve but an essential need. We'll talk more about that in chapter nine on inner health and strength.

I had to learn to look to myself to love myself. I had constantly sought approval and respite in other people, wanting them to feed and fill my emotional needs. That always left me disappointed. It's unrealistic to look to others to fill this for me. Only God can mend my heart. Through his love for me, I can learn to love myself and not be dependent on other people to fill me.

Accepting God's Compassion

How do we learn to accept this gift of compassion from God? We need to understand that it comes without conditions. He will help us learn how to change for the better. Let's look at a few references from Scripture to see this.

- Ps. 86:15 *"But you, O Lord, are a God of* **compassion** *and mercy, slow to get angry and filled with unfailing love and faithfulness."*

- Ps. 103:8 *"The Lord is* **compassionate** *and merciful, slow to get angry and filled with unfailing love."*

I love both sides of this description: "slow to get angry" and "filled with unfailing love." After having spent many years walking on eggshells around a man with an extremely quick temper, anyone who is slow to get angry feels like an immense blessing. It even feels at times like more than I deserve. I was so completely brainwashed into believing that I was the cause of my husband's rage, and that I could somehow control it if I could manage to tiptoe around him.

"Slow to anger" reminds me of my father. He was such a patient man. What a blessing he was, like the tall fir tree holding steady amid the wind and rain around me. I knew I could count on him to be that steady all the time. That's how I see God here: calm, steady, and my place of refuge because he comes first with compassion and mercy.

Even better is the "filled with unfailing love" side of this description. I'm not sure I can accurately picture what unfailing love looks like on this side of heaven, but the more I lean into God, the more I can begin to understand it.

What does that feel like if I really open my heart to it? To truly be loved with an unfailing love. Amazing, complete, fulfilling, whole. Finally, my heart can stop its constant searching for fulfillment, because I have finally found what I was missing.

- Mt. 9:36 *"When he saw the crowds, he had **compassion** on them because they were confused and helpless, like sheep without a shepherd."*

- Ps. 77:9-12 *"Has God forgotten to be gracious? Has he slammed the door on his **compassion**? Interlude. And I said, 'This is my fate; the Most High has turned his hand against me.' But then I recall all you have done, O Lord; I remember your wonderful deeds of long ago. They are constantly in my thoughts. I cannot stop thinking about your mighty works."*

At first Psalm 77 seems like a contrast to the others on compassion, asking if God has forgotten us and shut us out. We spiral into believing God turned against us and we have lost hope. Until we remember what he has done.

Suddenly we cannot stop thinking about his works and how much he loves us. What great compassion that he does not take offense at our doubt and constant loss of hope. Instead, he brings to mind all he has done for us, reminding us how we know we can trust him.

> Is. 30:18 *"So the Lord must wait for you to come to him so he can show you his love and **compassion**. For the Lord is a faithful God. Blessed are those who wait for his help."*

I love how this verse expresses God's compassion, in how much he wants to show his love for us, but that he waits for us to come to him. He doesn't force us to love him, but he can't wait to shower us in love and compassion once we turn to him. We are blessed when we wait for his help. How often I forget these truths and try to go out ahead of him.

> Ps. 79:8 *"Do not hold us guilty for the sins of our ancestors! Let your **compassion** quickly meet our needs, for we are on the brink of despair."*

I can think of many examples where abuse has carried through generations, often unknown to the children who are experiencing it. If they learn their own parents experienced similar trauma in their childhood, they can start to see their perpetrators with more compassion. This doesn't excuse the behavior, but they can understand their parents were hurt as well.

When I think about the generational impact, I'm reminded how desperately we all need Jesus in our lives to heal us. We can't do this alone. He can heal generations' worth of hearts and stop the continued destruction, if we allow him to change our hearts.

> Ps. 51:1 *For the choir director: A psalm of David, regarding the time Nathan the prophet came to him after David had committed adultery with Bathsheba.* "Have mercy on me, O God, because of your unfailing love. Because of your great **compassion**, blot out the stain of my sins."

For many of us our biggest failures are our own sins. This is where we need God's compassion the most, and where it feels the most gracious. God is always willing to forgive and give us compassion when we repent. We just have to be willing to ask for his forgiveness.

When Did the Lord Have Compassion for Me?

We've looked at the times in Scripture where God had compassion, but what about your own life? Remember, he doesn't just extend compassion in the stories in Scripture, but he extends compassion to each of us. Take a look at your own life.

What are the times when you feel God has had the most compassion on you?

If you're struggling, look at your life in age blocks. When was God compassionate to you as a child? When did he rescue you in your teens or twenties? When has he had compassion on you as an adult?

Write them down in your journal and thank God for his compassion. Below are a few of my examples.

1. Jesus sacrificed his life for me long before I was ever born, because he knew I would need it, so I could have relationship with him.

2. God gave me find friends to talk to when I was lost and confused and felt alone.

3. God continued to love me and protect me through every bad decision I made.

4. God gave me a little time with Dad before he was gone. He consoled me in my grief when we lost him.

5. God allowed me to have impact on women's lives even though I was still learning how to heal.

6. He healed me from my wounds. He stood beside me in my heartache, and slowly led me out of it. He allowed me to wallow, to rebel, to be stubborn, and still loved me through it.

Are there times you don't feel you deserved God's compassion? Can you allow yourself to accept his compassion in those areas of your heart you're still holding back from him? I hope you can open your heart and say yes to him, say yes to the compassion he's offering you.

Compassion in Leadership

What are some practical ways you can take compassion into your daily life? This can look like helping a neighbor or a family member with a project or bringing over a meal when they're tired or ill. It can be hearing where they are struggling in their lives and approaching them with understanding.

When we talk of compassion as a leader or in the workplace people often hesitate. That's the area we need to be firm on boundaries and rules, so everyone is treated fairly and performs as expected—at least that's what we're taught.

I would ask you to consider a different example. I had a young employee who had worked for the previous manager but stayed on when I took over the kitchen. He was hired as a dishwasher but also had an interest in learning how to cook. The previous manager had started teaching him more roles in the kitchen.

I heard his interest and started utilizing him in other areas as opportunities arose. He was really good at making grits for breakfast, and since I was a Northwest girl, grits were something I hadn't even tasted, nor knew how to prepare.

I normally tried to let the kitchen staff come as late as possible in the mornings, because it was always early hours. But I needed them to be on time and ready to work with that type of arrangement. They understood the requirement and most performed in appreciation of that schedule.

This employee had been late several mornings in the last couple weeks. I had expressed my displeasure each time he was late and asked him to be on time in the future. Some days he gave me a flippant attitude about it. That morning, he showed up about twenty minutes late. I asked him to get on the grill and help but told him I didn't want to talk to him until later.

I had made up my mind that it was too much. He'd been late too many times, and I couldn't rely on him. His attitude was a detriment to the team. I was ready to let him go. I think he knew that's how I felt.

When I met with him, he begged me to give him one more chance. He understood he'd left me in a lurch and was being disrespectful. He really needed the job and wanted it. I re-emphasized why it was important for him to be on time, for me to be able to rely on him, and that I needed his attitude to improve as well.

I could have chosen to continue with my plan to let him go. I had sufficient reasons to fire him. Instead, I gave him compassion. One more chance, but definitely his last chance, to prove to me he wanted this job and could be responsible.

I was glad I did. He turned around overnight. From that moment forward he was a hard-working, amiable, respectful, and most importantly, reliable employee. He continued to take on additional responsibilities and broaden his skills. He was friendly and liked learning new things. He became a strong asset and a motivator for the rest of the team.

If I hadn't been willing to show him compassion, he wouldn't have had the opportunity to grow and be responsible. I'm glad I was able to give him that chance. That's what we want for everyone in our lives, the chance to grow and become better people.

Seeing others with the compassion they need can give us the opportunity to show them grace and compassion, just like God did for us. Next, let's consider how compassion can contribute to our ability to live with courage.

Chapter 6
Embracing Courage

Courage can feel bigger than ourselves and like more than we know how to accomplish. But courage isn't one big moment. The only way we achieve being courageous is by the many small decisions we make every day. Each choice that stretches us when we're uncomfortable is a mini version of stepping out in courage. It's the many small moments that teach us how to act when we're faced with the big moment. The cumulative effect of many small choices will move us in the direction we want to go.

A lot of people have a misconception that they can't learn courage. They believe it's only an innate characteristic. But God doesn't limit us that way and I'm living proof that that's not the case. Although I had lost some courage during my marriage, I learned how to be courageous again after my divorce. Courage is a skill we learn and can re-learn throughout our life.

As a child we need to see courage modeled for us before we know how to do it for ourselves. Parents encourage children to take their first steps by showing them how to do it and encouraging them to try it for themselves. Then they stand there in support while the child tries.

Consider the small choices I made that taught me courage. I was very shy as a child, and I struggled with my shyness throughout grade-school and middle school. I didn't like to speak up in class even though I was a smart kid. This was something my parents couldn't model for me, since they hadn't learned either.

In high school, my dad pushed me into public speaking. He admitted he still struggled with his own shyness, and it had limited his ability to speak up in meetings at work. He didn't want me to struggle with it all my life like he had.

I had a teacher who taught me how to speak and forced me to practice—first in front of him, then in increasingly larger groups. So courage looked like stepping out of my shyness and speaking to a crowd. I hated it at first but learned to love it. I finally felt comfortable speaking my mind.

After high school, courage was attending the big Ivy League college across the country from where I grew up, because it offered me the greatest opportunity. I'd gotten into several colleges that were closer to home and more reasonably priced. But the lure of an Ivy League education and a scholarship was too much to pass up.

It was the first time I had launched out to a new place where I didn't know anyone. The academics were challenging. But both taught me what I could do when I stretched myself, skills I would continue to utilize.

In my late teens and twenties, courage was managing commercial kitchens and supervising crews of three to ten people. I got an early opportunity because the manager I trained under needed to step down for health reasons. This started with managing colleagues who were a few years younger than me for one meal a day but quickly turned into managing the whole kitchen.

I have my parents to thank for always encouraging me to take the opportunities set in front of me, knowing I could look to them for counsel when I had questions. I was trained by excellent managers, which also gave me the confidence to step into their shoes. This training set me up for success throughout my career. Both did an excellent job of teaching me how to be courageous one small action at a time.

We Were Taught Fear

But let me take you a step back and explain how I lost that hard-earned courage. I knew how to be courageous in my career but growing up with self-condemning beliefs had left a crack in that veneer when it came to my own self-worth. Courage didn't look like standing up for myself when someone put me down. That I swallowed and accepted. The lack of courage for myself left me susceptible to a backwards spiral in my relationships.

Being married to and living with a narcissist became a pattern of walking on eggshells. I was used to getting screamed at for the small inconveniences, so I did everything in my power to "handle" the details of plans, taking care of the chores, all the things that could spark a fit of rage.

One afternoon at work my husband screamed at one of my employees because they were keeping me late working through their questions, and he wanted me to leave and spend time with him. For some reason, he felt justified in unleashing his ten-minute tirade on my employee, displaying what looked more like a toddler's tantrum than an adult's disappointment.

There were no bounds to the amount of shame and embarrassment I felt at that moment. But keeping up the mask of "normal and okay" was still my first reaction. I explained to my employee how he had a quick temper. He'd get angry, blow off steam verbally, and then he'd be fine in a couple minutes. I apologized for his behavior, even though it was not mine to own.

For those of us who have been through trauma, we live in fear of events like these that triggered our abuser. I faced enough emotional trauma every day to make me want to retreat to a quiet corner, rather than believe I could do something new and adventurous.

I started to be afraid of everything. I didn't realize how quickly I could unlearn the courage I had worked for in my teens and twenties. But it didn't take an abuser very long to teach me fear. My body knew I was always on edge and sick at heart, but it took me years to consciously acknowledge it.

Enduring this abuse taught me to live in shame or fear and to hide from the world around me. I had spent so many years listening to the manipulation tactics that I no longer believed in myself or my freedom to make another choice. I was emotionally beaten down, unable to make decisions, always wanting to defer myself to everyone else's needs or desires.

It's hard to face the damage of being lied to for years causing our self-esteem to strip away. We've heard so many lies spoken over us that we eventually believe them. There came a point where I didn't recognize myself. I had become someone else to please everyone else. On my own, I didn't have the willpower to change.

In the midst of the trauma, I awoke one morning to a vision. I could see God reaching down into the muddy pit of my shame and despair to offer me a hand, a way out. I could hardly believe this could change, but I took his hand. With his strength and my willingness to climb, he pulled me out of that pit.

It was a slow climb out, and I was covered in muck and mire when I reached the top. But I was standing on solid ground next to my pit. Finally, I felt free. I didn't know what the journey looked like in front of me, but it was a gift that gave me hope. That moment of willingness was my first step towards the courage I needed to change, the courage to walk away from my abuser and start over again, alone in my forties.

Finding Courage

I needed that insight from God to give me the strength to get started. A small vision that gave me hope for a different future in front of me, and to know he was going to help me find my way there. But even with the vision, I needed time to evaluate the way my life was going to change.

I didn't instantly have the courage to change. It would take me a while to truly walk away. I wanted to wallow in my fear a little longer. It would turn my life upside-down if I chose a new life for myself. Was I strong enough? Could I trust God enough? I wrestled with my fears; I wasn't sure I had the strength to start again. Gaining back my courage would take time.

I had lived in the cycle of abuse long enough that it felt familiar, and on some days bearable. My energy was sapped; I was overwhelmed and so tired. But then another rough day, another fit of rage, or another time of being blamed for something I didn't do was enough to make me reconsider.

But God wouldn't let me forget that he had offered me a path out. I couldn't see where it was leading, and I hated the uncertainty. But I knew I couldn't continue with what I was doing—living a "normal" life on the outside and losing myself in the process.

I finally realized I had to stop letting others choose the direction my life was going. I had to learn to love myself again. I had to give myself enough respect to listen to what is important to me. I had to realize I was worth fighting for. I had to stop settling for good enough. And I couldn't wait any longer.

I made the choice to walk away from my marriage and home. I had to daily ask God for strength to survive the last few weeks of my marriage. I stayed in hotels and B&Bs to conserve enough energy to pack my belongings in our house every evening while enduring the blame and guilt my husband continued to pour on me. But God gave me the strength I needed for each day. He continued to sustain me and lead me out.

But I wasn't fully out yet. I didn't get it right that time. It takes me a while to learn. After my divorce, I started dating another narcissist and didn't give myself time to heal. But God didn't let me stay there. He got me alone during and after the pandemic where I finally allowed him to speak to my heart. He put strong counselors and good friends into my life.

I had to re-learn courage for myself. I had to practice the small steps, trust myself to step out in fear on the first step and believe in something better than what I had in front of me. I had to try the little things first—going somewhere new, eating out alone, and being willing to meet new people.

I had to evaluate my scenario and realize I was still trapped in another unhealthy relationship that was never going to change, until I made a choice to change it. It was like a bend in time. My partner was never going to value me in the relationship until I chose to leave. The two things should not have been tied together, but they inexplicably were.

I finally chose God and myself first. I moved back to the Northwest, where I knew God had led me fifteen years earlier. I opened my heart to possibility again and continued to seek his direction. I gave myself the time to grieve the life I had hoped for, and time for my heart to heal.

Then I was able to take the bigger steps in courage. Buying a house on my own. Changing jobs from a salaried employee to a consultant so I had more potential and less security. In all these steps, I continued to learn to step out in courage, and to place greater trust in God to always take care of the details, usually in an even better way than I imagined.

By leaning into his Word and his truth I began to see my value again. I learned to forgive myself. Learning to start life over again has been a continuous step of faith. Every day I have to trust again that he has more for me in this life, a bigger plan. I have to be willing to believe in him. I have to have the courage to say no to my former ways, and step into trusting him.

Making Choices

My choices may not be the same choices you needed to make for your situation, but I'm sure you had to make a choice to change as well. What did you have to walk away from in your life? What did God give you the strength to face? Where did you have to lean on him for the courage to take the next steps forward for your life?

Choosing to value ourselves is the first step in finding our courage. You've taken that first step. You've already walked away from your trauma as a survivor and chosen your healing journey over staying stuck in what was holding you back. You can continue to be more courageous.

Whether we realize it or not, we learned courage when we walked away from our trauma and chose a different life. And by knowing how to act with courage once, we can do it again. We can step out in faith, and we can do it afraid.

Remember the moment you chose to make a better life for yourself. Did you consider the ramifications that could impact your kids, your family, and your own life? You know what it is to weigh the pros and cons and make the right decision. It wasn't a choice you made carelessly, it wasn't easy. But you took that step forward even though you were scared and didn't know what the future held.

That's the reminder I have to tell myself often. It's okay to be afraid. I can still step forward and choose to be courageous even when I'm scared. The more we practice, the easier it is to do it again. We have to continue to walk closely with the Holy Spirit and lean into his leading. He can help bolster our courage to follow where he wants us to go.

Finding courage is actually a series of choices. Once we know our values and what we want to stand up for in our own lives, we can start choosing that every day. It starts with the small things. That's how we learn new habits. We can choose what we'll allow to influence our children's lives, even when we're facing pressure from family or friends.

We can have the courage to stand up for ourselves in our relationships. Our feelings and opinions matter. We can say no to inappropriate conversations at work. We can refuse to cover for other colleagues' irresponsibility. We can express our feelings and values to our parents and respectfully decline advice.

Sometimes I have to get a bit angry before I'm willing to stand up for myself. It's when I reflect on a situation and how it doesn't fit my values or beliefs that I can get angry enough to remember I have rights here as well. There are times I have to get angry to stay in the fight. It's easy to listen to the lies whispered over me, rather than standing in courage for what I believe in and what I believe about myself.

Many times, the next step in courage we learn is to set boundaries. This is always hard. It takes courage to make the best choice for your life when that choice also impacts the people around you.

But boundaries are often what we need for our mental and emotional health. Stepping out in courage meant I had to learn to express what was important to me and not feel guilty about it. I had to stop listening to the naysayers and people who didn't want me to change.

The struggle with boundaries is you have to set consequences or they're not boundaries. Otherwise, they're empty ultimatums. It takes courage to hold your ground. For the people pleaser in us, this can be gut-wrenching. It's something we have to practice repeatedly until we get better at it. It may not feel comfortable, but we will feel the benefit of the change in our lives.

Learning to manage people in our lives is a lot about managing expectations. You have to set clear expectations up front and then learn to maintain the boundaries that are defined by those expectations in order to bring success.

Principles of Boundaries as a Leader

As leaders, boundaries are important to maintain the expectations we set for our team. Setting boundaries allows us to determine the kind of culture we want to have in our group, organization, or workplace. We set a standard for attitude and behavior that drives how we interact with each other.

I found standing up for others was easier than standing up for myself. Right and wrong were more black and white for me when someone else was impacted. One clear boundary with my team was to always treat others with respect. This extended to how other people were allowed to treat them as well.

One afternoon my employee, let's call her Melanie, was going to out-brief a project team from their internal audit. The project team had not performed well in the audit and had been contentious throughout the process. I knew the out-brief would not be easy. I had another appointment, so had warned Melanie I would join the meeting a little late.

As I was leaving my appointment, two different colleagues asked me to join the meeting quickly, telling me the project team was verbally beating up Melanie, and she needed rescuing. I immediately joined the meeting.

My hackles were up, and I was ready to defend her. I had no hesitation knowing that she didn't deserve this sort of treatment. She had done the work, she was fair in her assessment, we had reviewed the data together before she concluded her results.

It wasn't easy to step in and shut down those who were beating her up, but it was simple. It was a must. No one deserved to be beaten up by a team who was defensive over the poor work they had done and were trying to place blame on the auditor rather than accept their own lack of performance.

I took control of the meeting and told them they were not allowed to speak to Melanie that way, and if they wanted to discuss it further, they could talk to me. I heard a few of their concerns, defended Melanie's results, and quickly ended the meeting.

In each of the following meetings to work through their corrective action plans, I attended to ensure there were no additional disagreements. I didn't hesitate in my resolve to ensure Melanie was supported and defended.

Having the courage to defend someone else didn't require any thought, it was the right thing to do. If I could do that for my team, I could certainly do it for myself. I deserved it as much as anyone else did. I just needed to remind myself of that truth.

Courage Takes Compassion

To step forward in courage we have to give ourselves compassion for the times we once held back in fear. We have to take our struggles to God and be willing to trust him to take care of them for us. He knows our fears already, but he wants us to bring them to him in faith.

Sometimes he takes us to the edge of our fear so we can see if we really trust him, with our whole heart. When we hesitate, we want to beat ourselves up in condemnation rather than giving ourselves grace. This isn't how God responds to us, so it shouldn't be how we treat ourselves.

God gives us compassion, and he wants us to have compassion for ourselves. God's love is so great for us. We can't imagine the depth of his kindness and compassion over us when we hold back in fear or when we make poor choices. Our own mindset is an instant condemnation, but he sees nothing but compassion for the heartache we're feeling.

If we open our hearts to him, we can allow that love to enter our own hearts and to speak compassion over our lives. We have to give ourselves that compassion so we can respond with the repentance God offers us. Compassion is what allows us to forgive ourselves.

Forgiving ourselves is the beginning of being able to forgive others and have compassion on others. That compassion allows us to see the heartache in others and have compassion for what they have been through. This is where we have to remember to be compassionate with ourselves and remember that sharing our lives with others is a benefit to both them and us.

Allow compassion for yourself and others to rule your heart. It takes courage for us to offer compassion to ourselves and to others.

Our self-compassion is what allows us to have courage to stand up for ourselves. We hold back based on fear of other's responses, when we need to be gracious enough to accept ourselves as we are, and show our authentic self to the world.

Once we are strong enough to believe in ourselves, we can step forward in courage to share ourselves with the world. This is what we want to model for those we're leading. But like us, they may need help learning how to be courageous.

Taking Courage into Leadership

We often have to teach courage to those we're leading. For the last corporation I worked for, one of the requirements for my team was to train and certify employees in management principles and guideline compliance, before they could qualify for new jobs they wanted to take on. These classes could be very interactive with the students. We also taught large training sessions open to all personnel in management roles.

For most of my team, teaching a large class was scary. I routinely reviewed my team's presentations and made suggestions. We would dry run their teaching until they were comfortable enough to understood the material and be prepared for questions that might come up.

I would attend the training my team taught so they had me to lean on if a question was difficult for them to answer. But I didn't let them off the hook or teach for them. They were more than capable. They just didn't feel comfortable in it. Pushing them to be courageous and face their fear taught them how to take small steps forward.

A few of them got good at teaching and enjoyed it, some even moved into roles where teaching was their primary responsibility. Some of them didn't learn to love training, but they did learn how to train routinely and how to have more confidence in front of a crowd. They learned courage with help, training, and practice.

While this fear of teaching a large audience can be tough to face, it's not the scariest thing your team will do. We can teach courage to our team. In the same way we had to learn courage by taking small steps and practicing courage, we can teach others.

Start by putting them in smaller scenarios, with smaller decisions that have less impact. Let them choose and face the consequences of their choices. Help them understand if they held back in fear or if they stepped forward with courage. Keep expanding the responsibilities they're given so they can continue to grow.

Consider making a business decision that will impact your team. As a leader you also have to weigh the consequences for those around you when you make your choices. That responsibility can feel weighty. But it's a good weight. God believes in you for the responsibility he has handed you.

But we have to remember that we know how to do this. We can give ourselves grace for our emotions. Then we can weigh the options and make the best decision for the most people. We don't need to be paralyzed with indecision. We can make the choice that allows our courage to shine through. God has given us the mind to make a decision, we can stand in his strength.

Taking our decisions before God will help us see his heart. Once we know we're following the direction God is leading, we can stand in faith instead of fear. It does get easier over time. God will give us the strength we need for each decision, for each day.

As leaders, we want to model courage for our team. It's okay to admit we're scared, but we need to model how we let God handle the details and don't hold back in our fear. As long as we're listening to the Holy Spirit, he will guide our steps and protect us from the wrong decisions. We learned courage by watching those in our lives step out in faith. We need to be that model for those around us.

As we step forward in courage, we are willing to change our lives. Often this means we need to evaluate where we're at and make a choice that moves us in the direction we're intending. This is where we learned to pivot. Knowing how to pivot is crucial to your leadership and a skill you learned likely in your trauma.

Chapter 7
Learning to Pivot

Let's take a walk in our friend Leah's shoes. Her story is in Genesis 29. The Bible tells us in Genesis 29:17: "*There was no sparkle in Leah's eyes, but Rachel has a beautiful figure and a lovely face.*" We're not sure if that alludes to a disfigurement of Leah's eyes, but we know based on the rest of the verse that Rachel was the most beautiful of the two sisters.

Leah was the oldest daughter, but her younger sister Rachel caught the eye of their cousin Jacob. Jacob was so enamored by Rachel that he agreed to work for her father, Laban, for seven years to earn her hand in marriage.

When it came time for the wedding, they celebrated with a feast with all their family and friends. But on their wedding night, Laban instead brought Leah to the bridal chamber once he had gotten the groom tired and tipsy from the day's activities. Unknowingly Jacob made love to Leah that night.

When Jacob awoke and found Leah in his bridal bed, he was angry and went to his father-in-law to demand the bride he had worked for: Rachel. Laban said it wasn't customary for the younger daughter to marry first, so insisted he stay with Leah for the bridal week and then he would give him Rachel as well, as long as he promised to work for him for another seven years.

A week later Jacob is given Rachel, and Jacob loved Rachel much more than Leah. How Leah's heart must have broken. First she lived much of her life in Rachel's shadow, next her father used her to trick her husband, and then she was rejected by her husband the morning after the wedding.

Still, Leah is favored with children and brings Jacob many sons. With each of the first three sons she tries to earn Jacob's love. We see this in how she names her sons: Rueban (*"The Lord has noticed my misery, and now my husband will love me"*), Simeon (*"The Lord heard that I was unloved and has given me another son"*), and Levi (*"Surely this time my husband will feel affection for me, since I have given him three sons!"*) (Ge. 29:32-35).

It is with the fourth son, Judah, that Leah chooses to praise God (Ge. 29:35). Somewhere between Simeon and Judah, Leah has changed her perspective on her situation. She has finally turned it over to God. Putting God first, instead of her husband's approval, changed her life.

Through his life, Leah's son Judah ushered in greatness for the kingdom of God. He fathered the tribe of Judah, which Jesus was born into. With her fourth son, Leah became the great-great-great grandmother of "the Lion of Judah." The Lion who conquered was born from a heart that had returned to God, no longer looking for praise from a man.

Leah gives us a great example of pivoting her life. She chose to stop focusing on earning her worth through her husband and instead chose to praise God for all he had given her. This change began her legacy.

Pivoting from Trauma

As a trauma survivor, you know what it is to pivot in your life like Leah did. No matter what trauma drove you there, the moment you chose to change your life is the moment you moved forward. You changed where your life was headed and moved in a new direction. Even if it felt like there was no other choice, you made a choice. That was when you learned to pivot.

But let me also acknowledge pivoting isn't as easy as our logical minds tell us it should be. Take today for example. I'm standing here on what feels like the edge of a precipice, about to make a six-figure financial decision that will radically change my life while also launching a book.

I'm trying to remind myself that pivoting is just evaluating the details and making a choice to move in a more promising direction. The last few days, as I was seriously considering putting in an offer, have felt like a roller coaster ride, and I hate roller coaster rides. They scare me, they tie my stomach in knots, they make me want to stop the ride and get off.

The trouble is I got on this ride voluntarily. And I want the result I expect at the end—the whirlwind exhilaration of having survived the ride. Then using that exhilaration to propel me into the next ride. But life-changing decisions should feel that way. Completely unsettling and concurrently totally exciting.

You see today I'm choosing to walk forward in faith and choose the new life God has handed me. I'm choosing to step into the ministry he designed for me. I believe I'll be able to reach people in a different way, which is why God chose this for me. It doesn't allow me the security of sitting back and playing it safe, it forces me to trust him to provide for me and for my employees daily.

I'm taking on a business that needs growth to succeed because I believe in its potential, and my own potential. I know I will need to change the strategy to bring in more revenue. I have many ideas on how that could work. I have to reach new clients and take the business in some new directions.

I wanted this dream to come easily. I hoped it would be a gentle stroll in the park with God by my side, easing into the new direction he has for me. God has been walking beside me every step of the way, holding my heart through the long season of waiting, keeping me encouraged and preparing me.

What surprised me was this pivot has felt like a quick left turn. I'd seen a couple warning signs but hadn't really clued in how near the turn was. But a quiet voice told me to look, and I did. I was expecting to buy a building, go through a remodel, and then open it to the public.

Instead, I'll be purchasing a bakery that's been open for a couple years, so getting started will be much faster. It feels like the turn suddenly led me into an open view that I didn't expect. I want to pull over a minute and take in the wonder before me. This is the opportunity I had asked for but in a way that I didn't predict, so it was taking me a moment to adjust.

But I'm ready to move forward. Even though it feels quick, it's the right time. I'm hanging on to this roller coaster for dear life. I'm terrified, but I'm doing it.

You can choose to pivot in your life too. There may be a dream you want to pursue that you didn't believe was possible. You may want to learn something new in your life or make new friends.

Pivoting is changing the direction of motion. You can change the trajectory in front of you because you have the power to make that choice. Your trauma taught you that you were capable and enough to handle unexpected shifts.

The ability to pivot is an important skill set for your life. It allows you to assess a situation and choose how to handle it. You get to decide what result you want to see and the best way to get there. You don't have to accept what life hands you with no ability to influence it. This ability is key to your success in all areas.

> Not everyone can pivot; only survivors do.

Not all survivors are developed out of trauma, but many of us are. You have the mindset to believe in yourself and to believe in something better for your life. You know you have the freedom to make a choice. Pivoting can require us to give ourselves compassion and require courage to face our fears. We know these are abilities we've already learned, we just have to keep utilizing them. You can change the direction of your life. What do you want to change in your life? How can we use this skill for our benefit?

Learning How to Pivot

Let's look at how to pivot, using pivoting in business as an example we can apply to our lives. When we look at a business, we think of a company enacting a significant change to their core operations, their products, or their services. In our personal lives, pivoting is changing the core of who we want to be, and how we want to show up in the world. Even if you're not dreaming of a business or in one right now, there are several similarities between business and personal that you can still apply to your situation.

We want to be a different person than we were, or we want to achieve something we didn't believe we could do. We want to become a stronger, better person because we want to set an example for our children or families. We want to be an example to people around us in our community.

So how do we do it?

    1. **Pivot as soon as you can**. (Founder Institute, 2023)[1]

In business, pivoting quickly is encouraged to increase profit or cash flow, especially if a business is in trouble. But it should always

---

1. *Founder Institute*. (2023, April 26). Retrieved from fi.co: https://fi.co/insight/what-pivoting-is-when-to-pivot-and-how-to-pivot-effectively

be approached with enough research to ensure there is predicted success in the change being made, rather than flailing at any idea that comes to mind.

Throughout my career, I've worked for non-profit organizations, as well as large for-profit corporations, and owned several small businesses. In each case there is still a need to drive increased revenue and cash flow, just the purpose that revenue is used for differs depending on the organization. The philosophy is the same whether you're selling a product or a service: continue to drive more customers to utilize your offering.

Maybe your business is experiencing seasonal gaps in sales or utilization, and you need to evaluate how you can appeal to your clientele in the off-peak season. You'd want to evaluate how you could change your product to appeal in different seasons. You would want to see if there's a similar clientele based that you haven't reached yet.

Where in your personal life should you consider a pivot? Does your current job no longer motivate you? Have you taken on too much responsibility in your home rather than asking for help? Have you stayed in a friendship that's become a gossip session rather than a supportive network? Are you hanging onto a relationship that's unhealthy for you?

In these scenarios, for your own mental and emotional health, you should evaluate what is causing you to accept scenarios that don't make you happy. Then you need to change as quickly as you can to minimize the continued heartache or discontent. This doesn't mean you have to run from a relationship because it isn't all healthy for you. Often in these scenarios, it looks like putting limits on time spent with someone who's difficult or being able to speak up for yourself about how you're feeling. It may be asking for additional responsibilities or challenges at work or asking to share chores at home.

Maybe you have a goal you've wanted to achieve for a long time, and you're motivated to get started. You want to move your life in a positive direction, and you've determined the best first steps that will make progress on that path. You'll be much more satisfied with your life once you start investing energy in making that change. The sooner you start, the better you'll feel.

2. Set new goals that align with your vision.

In business this looks like setting new profit or revenue goals based on the new strategy you're starting. It can be the number of people you're serving or the amount of products you sell. It can include time for a new product to reach consumers or a marketing campaign to have an effect. If you're a non-profit this could include a goal for donations received.

For your own life, this may look like reclaiming an hour of your day for you to take a walk, or have some quiet time. It may mean sharing the responsibilities with someone else so you have time to work on that goal you've been dreaming about. But it's important to establish a goal—and a goal that's obtainable.

This may look like fifteen minutes in your morning for quiet time to re-center your heart and mind before you start your day. It may look like thirty minutes a day to start a project you want to work on. It may look like not allowing others to speak words of negativity over you.

3. Focus on your progress and use what you've learned.

Pivoting doesn't have to mean turning in the oppositedirection and starting over. It can mean turning a little bit from where you were and re-focusing. For a business you may have the right product, but you missed marketing to a segment of your consumers. You may have learned that your product needs to change a little to be more effective for more consumers. You may want to branch your offering platforms to reach a broader audience.

In our own lives this can be how we frame our progress. We may have spent some time researching our new goal, only to find we need to approach it from another way. That doesn't mean we wasted the time doing the research. That research gave us more insight into the new direction we want to head. We can evaluate the best path forward and move in that direction.

We may find we're not making progress as quickly as we'd hoped or seeing the results we expected. But we don't want to get discouraged. This is where evaluating what's working and not working can help us see where we've had success and give us pointers about where we need to make a small shift to increase our progress or productivity.

4. Listen to feedback.

In business your feedback is from your customers. How much of a product or service are they purchasing? What is influencing their purchase? How much is driven by market influences or effective marketing? Is it a product that they will purchase once or re-buy often? Can you offer a subscription for your product or service? What are customers telling you in your surveys about their satisfaction with your product?

In our lives this is being willing to receive feedback from those who matter to us. We can ask our spouse or a trusted friend what results they see from our efforts. We can evaluate for ourselves if our changes are impacting our schedules or our mental health. Maybe we're working with a mentor or coach and we can ask them to evaluate our progress. We can also listen to what guidance we're getting from the Holy Spirit to help us stay on the right course.

5. Ensure this pivot is moving you in the direction you want to go.

In business this can be more measurable. You can measure how much product you sell, how many people you've reached or what organizations you've made a difference in. You can measure if you're increasing your reach in that underserved group of people.

In your own life you need to evaluate if this pivot is moving you in the direction you want to be moving. Are there measurable results you can see, such as obvious progress or a change in your attitude? Are you enthusiastic about the change you're seeing or frustrated? This can help you determine if any adjustments are needed.

6. Develop a pivoting plan.

In business this looks like defining what your new product is, who all your customer groups are, what your marketing strategy is. It can include delivery methods and seasonal fluctuations in your customer base. Then you can define short-term and long-term goals for product success.

In your own life this begins with how you will measure your success, which also includes defining what success is for you. Then you need a plan for how you're going to get there. I recommend taking a small piece of a bigger goal you want to achieve, breaking it down into something that's manageable. Then define how you're going to take a small action towards that each day. This also makes it easier to measure your success.

Your plan may be to take fifteen minutes for mindfulness each morning. You can measure this first by your success at taking this action each day. But you can also measure its effectiveness over time. Are you more centered in your approach each day because you took time for mindfulness? Are you calmer in how you respond to issues that arise?

If your plan is standing up for yourself and setting a boundary for how folks treat you, this may start with small interactions with people and build up to how you learn to respond to that person who is super frustrating in your life. Have you seen a change in how they respond to you? Is there a change in your attitude towards the other person?

Your plan may include career growth or searching for a new role that will be more challenging. You can measure this with how many opportunities you're gaining in your current role or additional skills you're learning. Changing your career can start with updating your resume and submitting to new jobs each week.

7. Communicate the pivot.

For a business this begins with internal communication with their own teams to ensure everyone is on the same page with where their focus needs to be going forward, and how this new product or strategy will reach the customer. It would include what the new goals are and what marketing is needed to reach the consumer.

Then it's communicating this to both investors and customers. Investors need assurance that they understand where the company is going and how this is going to be more successful. Then customers need to hear how your product or service has changed or expanded and how it will benefit them; why they need it. If your company is moving into a new market space or changing philosophies, it's important to clearly communicate why and how you're changing.

In your personal life this begins as an internal discussion with yourself. You need to buy into how you want to make progress or change your life. You have to believe in it for yourself first. You know this is something you want, and you believe this new approach or new strategy will help you achieve that change. You need to speak affirmations over yourself.

Then you need to share your plan with at least one trusted friend, someone who can encourage you or help hold you accountable to what you want to do. They can also share your excitement and encourage you. You may want to bring in a coach to help you, and you need to clearly define what you want to do and the progress you want to achieve.

This may also include communicating your change in priorities or plan to those it would most influence or impact in your circles. This can include explaining priorities and boundaries to friends and family so they understand why you're doing things differently than before. It may include changing your work schedule or how many extra projects you are willing to take one.

Taking the time to communicate with those closest to you why you are making this change can help you be successful. You can choose who you're ready to include in that circle. But being firm on your new plans will help strengthen your resolve.

8. Monitor and revise.

In a business this is a constant monitoring of the success of a product or service. You can measure this with sales, profit, or marketing campaign success. If it's working, you can continue in the same vein or even find ways to improve what you've started.

If it's not having the success you expected, you can fine tune what you're doing to continue to improve. In business you want to be careful that you aren't all over the place in defining yourself as a company, so you need to be strategic about your changes.

In your personal life you have more freedom to continue to change and improve, as long as it's all moving you in the direction you want to go. You get to continue to evaluate if this is where you wanted to go, and how you can continue to move further in that direction and improve.

It's your character and goals you're changing. You get to decide who you want to be going forward, what you what to invest your time and energy in, and how you want the world to see you. You get to have the influence you want on the world.

Change takes time. Celebrate the small wins and progress along the way. It will help keep you motivated to keep reaching forward for the next step, the next thing.

Ability to Thrive

Pivoting gives you the ability to survive, but also to thrive and to find the best in a scenario. You can continue to look forward and to make the best choice for you. You can set new goals and accomplish them. You can continue to change the trajectory of your life in a positive direction.

This skill is highly desirable for leaders. It's hard for many people to motivate themselves to do something different if what they're doing today is working. But you've seen what change has accomplished in your life, and you're willing to do it again if there's something you want to change.

You can utilize this skill to motivate others around you who may not be able to see a different path or figure out how to achieve it. They may be scared to change. It may sound too difficult. But you've seen the reward for working in a new direction and achieving your goals. You can lead them to a greater result, despite the fear.

So how do we continue to thrive? If you've felt like continuing to pivot is getting harder to do, I want you to see where your strength is for the journey. Next let's talk about how trauma taught us to persist in achieving our goals.

Chapter 8
Persistence and Endurance

I was talking with a friend last night about marriage. Both of us had married men who were alcoholics and new Christians. We both believed when we got married—and still do—that we're forgiven and new creations in Christ. But neither of us was familiar at all with the profound struggle alcoholism is for those who are addicted. Nor could we have predicted the impact it would have on our lives in the long term. We were both naïve, having never been exposed to anyone who battled addictions.

We talked through the disappointment of watching our husbands' relapses, as well as the heartbreak of watching it control their lives and eventually ours too. We talked about the many ways I tried to make my marriage work and the additional chances I'd given my husband.

Some of the examples were supporting him through the eighteen pre-trial months after he'd been at fault in a car accident. He spent many of those months in and out of drug and alcohol rehabilitation programs because he couldn't face his future. I also supported him through nearly three years in prison once it was determined he was guilty.

After he was released on parole, I found a new job in a new city to give him the opportunity to restart his life on better footing. He still managed to lose his job and spiral into a deep depression instead of looking forward to his future with hope.

I had supported him through all this, looking towards a future where he was healing and improving his life. I stayed by his side and continued to encourage him. I stayed committed to my marriage and believed we would weather these storms together.

That's where I fell on the wrong side of the fence. I had trusted my husband's words that he wanted to change, that he wanted to do better and improve his life. That was true, he did want those things.

What he didn't want to do was put in the time and effort it would require from him to make those changes in his life. He wanted it handed to him; he wanted it to be easy to change. We'd all like that scenario, but it's not reality.

I recognize now I was also enabling his bad choices by not allowing him to face all the consequences of his decisions. By continuing to clean up his messes and try to make everything appear normal to the outside world, I was encouraging him to continue in his ways. I wasn't helping the situation, even though I thought I was doing the right thing.

What I chose to ignore was the contrast between what he told me he wanted versus what he was willing to do. I saw that his actions were inconsistent, but I believed I should give him grace, continue to forgive and that he would improve in time, and I should be patient with the process. What his actions proved was he wasn't going to make the necessary changes to improve his life, or at least not now, and not with me.

For me there were beliefs that also limited what action I felt I could take. I had been brought up in a family that didn't believe in divorce. I was taught that you married once, for life, and you made it work, even when it was hard. Being committed to your partner through the ups and downs is important, as is their commitment to you. But at the time I didn't have room in my beliefs to handle abuse in the relationship.

These beliefs were embedded in me. Not only had I learned forgiveness and grace in church all my life, but I had also been programmed by a narcissist to defer my values to the other person in a marriage, placing the marriage itself higher in value than my own beliefs.

There is value to not allowing your own desires to control the relationship at every point. Often you do need to compromise for the health of your relationship. But what I was really doing was setting aside my values to ensure the marriage survived because I was afraid of abandonment. If I let the marriage fail, I'd be abandoned again, and that fear was insurmountable in my mind.

It made me realize that's something we learn as we healed from trauma—persistence and endurance. We can go through hard things and survive them and come out stronger on the other side. People can change their lives and make things better if they are committed to it and diligently work towards it. It's something we've proved to ourselves in our own healing.

Evaluating Persistence

Along the way we need to learn to segregate between what is healthy persistence and endurance and what becomes unhealthy. Healthy persistence can be very helpful in our own lives, or in the lives of those around us. But when it's unhealthy, it can enable someone else's bad behavior, which doesn't help them and often makes us sick at the same time.

There are several issues I've been describing here that can help us segregate when we've moved between healthy and unhealthy persistence and endurance. Let's take a look at these questions to evaluate our situations, and compare that to those around us that are more successful. We'll also learn to translate these questions into how we want to act in our relationships and as leaders.

1. What are our beliefs leading into the scenario?

2. What are our motives in the process?

3. What are the other person's actions telling us?

4. How would our friends interpret what's happening?

5. Are we afraid to ask for help?

6. Are we repeating a pattern from the past? Is it healthy?

7. What is God asking us to do in this scenario?

Let's explore each of these questions.

1. **What are our beliefs leading into the scenario?**

For me in my marriage, I firmly believed marriage was a one-time event in your life, no matter what, unless you were widowed. I believed all issues in marriage could be solved.

What that belief didn't allow for was a scenario where I was being used and abused. I was committed to making the marriage work even though my partner had checked out a long time ago. I tried very hard to continue supporting him through everything he was going through, even through the demise of my own mental, emotional, and physical health. At this point my endurance had outrun my clarity of vision about the health of my relationship.

In my case my beliefs pushed me over the edge into unhealthy territory. I do believe marriage is designed to be a one-time event in our lives, minus scenarios out of our control where one spouse survives the other. But it's not meant to be the altar we sacrifice our lives on. We don't have to be committed to unhealth in cases of abuse. (If this is an area you're struggling, please read Appendix A).

All issues in a marriage can be solved, if both partners are committed to God and to each other; and are willing to work on issues that arise because they're committed to the success of their relationship. What I had missed was the second half of the equation.

I believed that all things could be solved, without thinking how it would take both people investing in the relationship for it to succeed. Without having a willing partner, I took the whole burden of the marriage's success on my shoulders. Not only was I unsuccessful in that endeavor, I also took all of the blame upon myself.

When I look at healthy marriages around me, I see two partners who make each other the priority in their lives. They believe in the success of their marriage because they believe in the enduring commitment they have to each other. They work together as team, showing love to each other, giving each other companionship, and serving God together as a team. They can talk through differences in a safe place and find solutions.

Maybe you're facing a struggle with healthy versus unhealthy persistence with a family member or friend. What do you believe about this relationship? Do you believe you both are committed to a healthy relationship? Do you feel safe to express how you're feeling?

Evaluate if you are honoring the relationship out of obligation or desire. Your feelings will tell you if you're willing to listen to them. Dread or joy will reflect your mentality. Are you giving more than you are able out of guilt? You may need to stop pursuing someone who doesn't want your help or want to change.

2. What are our motives in the process?

In my marriage, my motives were unhealthy coming into the relationship. I couldn't recognize it at the time, but it's clearer in hindsight. I was very afraid of being abandoned. I'd gotten married in part because I didn't want to be alone, and I didn't see my value as an individual; I only felt worthy once I had gained the status of being married.

I didn't know how to deal with conflict and resolution in a healthy manner. I had been trained by a narcissist to never assert my own feelings into the situation, but to make sure that the narcissist's values were being served. I didn't have the tools to be able to express what I was feeling without laying blame onto my husband. I expected him to know my needs without me clearly expressing them, and I was frustrated when he didn't meet those expectations.

When I look at other marriages around me, I can see partners who are willing to deal with conflict because they know their relationship is secure and based in unconditional love for each other. They are willing to work through issues as they come up and openly talk to each other to resolve areas that need improvement.

Do you struggle with conflict resolution in other relationships—family or friends or even co-workers? This hesitation often carries through many of our relationships, but it can also tell you something if it's only one relationship in your life where it's a struggle.

At the same time, we can evaluate what we're doing to grow and encourage a relationship. Are we investing the time and attention a growing relationship needs? Do we take time to learn the other person's preferences and do things to show our appreciation? This can make a difference in any relationship.

Sometimes we've chosen to be in a relationship with someone because of what we believe we can gain from the relationship. It may be a subconscious desire for status or pride. We may befriend a co-worker to look better to our boss or to increase our likelihood of success.

This is where we need to take our motives to God and ask him to show us the truth in our hearts. I want to honor God in doing what he has laid on my heart to do. I want to fulfill the purpose God designed for me, not fulfill the goals I think are best for me, without his input. I want to ensure I put energy into healthy relationships and give to those where God is asking me to.

3. What are the other person's actions telling us?

I wasn't listening to what my husband's actions were telling me. I was also refusing to acknowledge reality. I wanted to live in the dream of what I hoped my spouse and our marriage could be, rather than assessing the reality in front of me.

I took his words at face value and believed them because I wanted to believe them. His actions were telling me he was continuing to return to his addictions rather than doing the work to stay sober.

What does a supportive relationship look like to you? Consider your relationship with friends or family and how the relationship feels to you. A relationship can feel very one-sided if only one person is investing in its growth. Do you see the other person investing in you? Do you feel heard and valued?

While you're working to change your future path, look to see who your biggest supporters and encouragers are. This will help direct you to the people that are on your team. They are willing to step up and find ways to help you succeed in this endeavor. They are willing to check in on your progress and keep you accountable.

4. How would our friends interpret what's happening?

When it came to my marriage, my friends were telling me I was in a bad situation, and I needed to get out of it. They could see my husband wasn't going to change and that I was enabling his bad behavior.

Even my parents apologized to me and told me they were wrong in teaching me to believe divorce was not an option. They gave me the freedom to make a different choice. I realized how much weight I had put on myself not to disappoint them when that weight was lifted.

My parents' willingness to give me my freedom spoke volumes over the situation I was in. For them to say they'd support me in leaving my husband meant it was bad—really bad. And it still took me time to see it.

I heard them, I agreed with them, and I still gave him more chances, because it took me a long time to let go. I still wanted to persevere; I allowed myself to stay in my fantasy land for much longer than I should have.

In a family or friend relationship, it may not be about leaving the relationship. It may look more like healthy boundaries. The same may be true with a co-worker. You may not be able to change jobs today, but you may be able to work towards that. Or you may have to learn how to express yourself more clearly in several relationships.

It helps you to listen to what the people around you are telling you. If they're hearing more than normal frustration from you, they may try to help you see where this relationship has moved from healthy to unhealthy. They may be expressing caution about something you were writing off as normal. Take the time to evaluate it with honesty.

Once you started making healthy changes in your life, how did your friends and family interpret those changes? Can they see you're improving your life? Their support of how you're making new choices and avoiding old patterns can be so motivating!

5. Are we afraid to ask for help?

I didn't want to ask for help with my husband's addictions. I didn't want to force him to be accountable to someone else. Not asking for help was a terrible choice for me. Because I was hiding behind what I was doing, I already subconsciously knew it was unhealthy. I was unwilling to admit it to myself or others.

I didn't want to admit my husband had a problem and I didn't know how to handle it. I wanted to paint the picture that everything was okay to everyone around us. My own pride got in the way of my health.

For any relationship, staying in good counsel is key. This can be the counsel of a good friend, a mentor, a pastor, or it can be a professional who can evaluate your situation with less bias. Over time, I've learned to be less concerned with what others think about me, and to be more concerned with my mental and emotional health.

I'd rather come to the table with honesty and have someone challenge me, than to live in unhealth. I spent way too many years in unhealth and being unwilling to examine my own motives—worse yet, allow anyone else to. But I understand that can feel overwhelming.

Good counsel can also look like those who are further along the path than we are. In a work environment we often shadow or are paired with someone with more expertise in our area so we can learn from them. We can do the same in our personal lives. Look for those people who you respect and ask for their counsel. If you see someone who's achieved a goal you're working towards, ask about their experience.

Today I'm learning I can ask for help and support when I need it. I may need a friend to step in and help if a project is taking more time than I expected. I can ask for help in how to break down a task into smaller pieces when I get overwhelmed. I can ask questions and research information to improve my understanding. I can allow others to perform tasks they have more experience in than I do.

I can ask for friends to help process the emotions I'm feeling and help me see my situations with more clarity. I can ask for them to partner with me in seeking God's direction. I don't have to do everything alone. God gave us community to lean on.

6. Are we repeating a pattern from the past? Is it healthy?

My marriage was repeating a pattern from the past, but I didn't recognize it yet. I hadn't evaluated my life enough to understand my mother was addicted to pain killers and had been since my teenage years. My subconscious knew there was something dreadfully wrong with this situation, but it hadn't yet reached my conscious brain to be able to put words to it.

I was able to predict every time my husband would relapse. I could feel or see the patterns even though I couldn't name them. I would start staying late at work to avoid going home because I knew he was spiraling. I didn't consciously know I was avoiding him. I did it because I could read his patterns and recognize when I didn't want to deal with him.

I may have even known he didn't have the strength to win the battle against his addictions. But then I would have had to admit my marriage was a failure, and that was too hard to do considering I had hung my own success upon the success of my marriage.

Are you repeating a pattern in your relationships that you learned in childhood? Do you take a particular role or position at work because it's an easy default? Do you allow an older sibling or a parent to convince you to do things you don't want to do? Consider where you may need to enact healthy boundaries.

For some of us there are healthy relationships in our lives we're working to exemplify. This may look like supportive parents who had healthy communication, and you're working towards repeating those patterns. You may have a great mentor at work that's coaching you in healthy career steps.

Consider what you want your future to look like. You can choose to stop repeating unhealthy patterns. You can identify and ignore the stumbling blocks of your past and find healthier ways to achieve your dreams. You can stay in close pursuit of God and his plan for your life.

7. What is God asking us to do in this scenario?

In the past, I couldn't hear what God wanted me to do. I wasn't listening. I was so lost in my own emotions and confusion I didn't know how to hear his voice. I was so used to hearing the manipulation and lies my ex-husband devised into a "reasonable" story, I no longer knew how to discern the truth.

Ask God to give you discernment over your relationships and your motives. He can help you understand when he's using you to help someone else and when you're learning in a relationship. He will also help you discern unhealth in a friendship or family dynamic, and he can show you what to do about it. Our job is to listen and obey.

I can continue to pursue God with my future. Leaning into him will help me set my sights on what he has for me. It will help me draw closer to him and to mold my heart to see the world like he does. He is asking me to trust him with the outcome.

Keeping Our Focus

Persistence and endurance can be two sides of the same coin. Most times we start from the right place. We love people, we want to encourage them, we want to believe in them, we want to support them in their growth. But it can quickly flip when we find we're doing the work for someone else, rather than encouraging them to improve themselves.

I point this out as a caution. The fact that we have endured so much hurt in our relationships makes us stronger people. It can also be a weakness if we don't check in with ourselves to ensure we're staying in healthy endurance. Becoming an enabler to someone else's bad choices will steal our health from us. We've worked so hard to get to this point, we have to protect ourselves from what can cause us to backslide.

Our emotional and mental health can be fragile if we don't nurture it. We'll get further into healthy practices in the next chapter, but I want to remind us to protect the health we've fought so hard for. It's okay to learn to care for ourselves and set boundaries with others.

We also have to learn to hear God's voice in and over our lives and our choices. Learning to take the time to be quiet and listen can be hard. Especially if the voices in our heads have been filled with condemnation up until recently. That isn't God's voice, that's Satan speaking lies to you. But we have to spend time in God's Word and in prayer to recognize his voice through the noise.

The key is where you set your hope. You can't set it on other people solely and hope they want to change. Your hope has to be in God, and in yourself through God's strength. The other person has to show they want to change too, not just in words but in actions. That's true of us too: we show who we want to be by our actions.

What's the greatest difference between healthy and unhealthy scenarios? Where the focus is. Keeping God's vision and his focus in our lives is the key to all success, in life and in relationships.

> Isaiah 26:3 says, *"You will keep in perfect peace all who trust in you, all whose thoughts are fixed on you!"* That peace comes from hearing his voice and staying within his plans for us. When it feels hard to know where God's leading you, take the time to lean into the quiet, meditate on his Word, and wait for him to answer you.

> Psalm 5:3 also says, *"In the morning, Lord, you hear my voice; in the morning I lay my requests before you and wait expectantly."* This verse reminds us to pray and wait expectantly. We don't wait, wondering if God heard us. We wait expectantly, knowing he heard and will answer. His way and his timing are always better than ours.

Trusting God is what will keep us moving forward into the future vision we have for ourselves, with his direction.

After looking at these examples, you can see why it's important to keep our focus on God to ensure we're following hard after the things he has for us, rather than our own desires. We need to continue to compare our beliefs to his Word to ensure we haven't gotten off course along the way. Persistence in health can help us to achieve the goals God has set in front of us.

Persistence in Leadership

Let's consider similar questions as we approach leading others.

Do we believe in our own abilities to lead? If we don't believe in ourselves first, we won't have the confidence necessary for others to believe in us. Do we believe we are skilled as a leader, and understand the organization or people we're leading? Evaluating our own skills and character can help us lead effectively and know when we need outside expertise.

Are our motives pure in wanting to lead? Do we desire to see people or organizations grow, or are we looking for the accolades that come from leading them into success? How is the group we're leading reacting to us? We want them to be endorsing us and supporting our efforts, we want to have earned their support.

Persistence toward organizational goals should look and feel rewarding. Do your closest advisors share in your enthusiasm for the organization's success? Check in with them to see if there's anything they see that needs adjusting.

Ask for help from your mentors, from your leaders, from your team. Don't try to take it all on alone. They're part of this organization because they want to be part of making the goals happen. Share that with them.

Persistence after the right things and listening for God's direction becomes even more important as you take on more leadership roles. Your choices will impact those around you so you want to be careful you're leading them in the right direction. It's crucial as a leader you're even more closely in tune with the Holy Spirit.

Leadership can feel like a lot of responsibility. It is. So how do we continue in healthy persistence while maintaining our own relational, mental, and emotional health? I'm glad you asked. Let's look at some ways to stay focused on our source of strength, as well as protect our health and our energy while we lead others.

Chapter 9
Inner Health and Strength

While writing this book, I struggled with a lack of energy. In part I was disappointed with the lack of progress towards my goals. The feeling made me question if I'm on the right path or if I heard God's voice clearly. I thought I had heard him clearly on the bakery as part of the ministry, but I wasn't finding a building or hearing from the owner on a building I hoped for. I didn't understand why.

I was making the right choices. I was leaning into God's Word, I was praying over it, wanting to continue to hear his direction. I was establishing good friendships with those who were strong in their faith and who could walk beside me and encourage me in this faith journey. I was voicing that vision to those around me for support, rather than hiding it and lacking the confidence to share it.

I felt he had clearly given me specific desires for working beside other women who wanted to change their lives. Every other door I tried to open, he closed or put it on my heart to walk away. And trust me, there were a lot of doors I tried to open. In hindsight, I felt like I needed to test every door to be sure this wasn't the one God had for me.

That's part of my nature. Keep pushing for the thing in front of me, run towards the vision so we can start it now. Ignore this in-between time where God's preparing me. I'm sure I'm ready already, because I'm so excited about what's coming. I had to learn to be patient in the waiting as well. To learn that while this time may feel unproductive, it's never unproductive with God.

I'm beginning to see the logic in his wisdom. Writing the book was harder than I expected, and starting a business will be all consuming. Assuming I could do both at once was optimistic. And the ministry needs the book at its foundation. It had to come first. As leaders, we have to be willing to wait on God's timing. Even though it's uncomfortable, even when we get discouraged. God's plan is so much bigger than we can see.

My own perspective on time comes from a scarcity mindset. I lost both my parents earlier than I should have, and neither was prepared for a shorter lifespan. I look at that and wonder how much time I have to accomplish the goals God has set on my heart.

I fear that I'm not getting any younger, and I may not be able to do some of the things I want to do if my health declines with age. What I tend to forget is that God knows the limits of my days. He set this goal in front of me, knowing how much time and energy I have available.

At the same time, I needed to be realistic about how to go about it. Pushing myself to fill every moment with what I felt was a "productive" use of my time was not how God designed it. There are many ways we can look at how to be more focused on God's plan and how to keep ourselves healthy in the process.

The most important thing to keep in mind as we look for the healthiest way to lead others is where our source of strength is. In our case that's WHO our source of strength is. Our focus has to first be on God and to stay close to his leading, so that we know we're staying in his path. We have to lean into him for our strength in order to lead others. There are many ways to do this.

Daily Practices

Morning Devotions and Prayer

We start with how we order our day. What daily practices do you have in place today to help keep you focused on God? We can set the tone for our day. It starts with our mornings; the first activities we take time for.

What do your mornings look like today? For me, my day doesn't start well unless I start the day with a devotional, some time in God's Word, and prayer. Maybe for you that also includes worship music.

I need to center my heart on the Lord first if I want to keep my focus on him throughout the day. When something throws off my morning schedule, I find the sooner I can take that time for him, the sooner I can reset to a place of peace.

The days before I took time for God first thing in the morning left me edgy and triggered as soon as I had to start dealing with other people in my day. I didn't have the strength and peace I needed in my own life to offer peace or hope to anyone around me.

Many times people aren't sure how to get started with morning prayer or a devotional. Or it feels intimidating to study God's Word on their own. There are two routes I recommend for getting started. With either option, first ask God to open your eyes and your heart to the message he has for you today.

The first option is to start with a devotional from an author you respect or focus on a topic that's near to your heart. I recommend one that's taking a verse or two and showing you how to apply that in your own life. In either case start by asking God to open your eyes and your heart to the message he has for you today.

Start with reading the devotional and meditating on how it impacts you, or what change it's challenging you to make in your life. If you have more time, take the verse that the devotional is based on and read that verse and a few verses near it in the Bible for context and to give you more to meditate on.

The other option is to start with a book in the Bible that you want to read. Read a few verses at a time, making sure to take in the context of what's happening at that time, what people's actions and reactions are, and what the words say. Then spend some time meditating on God's Word, how it applies to you today, and think about what God is asking from you in these verses.

After that, go to God in prayer. Take a few minutes to thank him for what he's done and what he's doing in your life. Ask him to point out areas in your life where you need forgiveness. Ask forgiveness for anything he brings to mind. Pray for those around you who need God in their lives. Then present to him what your needs or desires are. Ask him to lead and direct you throughout your day.

Continue the conversation with him throughout your day. When you're struggling to be patient with someone around you, ask him to guard your words and actions and to give you the patience to deal with someone with kindness and grace.

Give yourself grace while you're getting used to your new routine. Set your alarm fifteen minutes earlier to give yourself time to start your day this way. When you miss a day, don't beat yourself up about it, forgive yourself, and do better the next day or later that day. God is ready and eager to talk to you the minute you make time for him.

Self-Care

Taking time for yourself will always help your mental state. Your brain needs some downtime instead of running from event to event or from task to task. Allow yourself to take breaks. This can be a break from work, from caring for others, from serving too much.

It's not just about getting facials or manicures done, even though those can be a beneficial part of self-care if they help you relax. For many of us who were abused, we often set aside our own needs for the needs of others. A bit of self-sacrifice can truly help. But a lot of it can weary our souls at a deep level, especially if we haven't learned how to re-fuel ourselves.

Self-care doesn't have to be expensive or take hours away from your family. But it matters that we take the time. Even if that's fifteen minutes of calm alone time to re-center or a short walk to reset our nervous system. We can take a few minutes before bed to get lost in a good book to reward ourselves for a productive day.

Think about what restores you. Do you enjoy time with friends, or do you like to get away on your own? Do you feel refreshed spending time in nature or re-fueled by an evening out on the town? Does a day of pampering yourself sound heavenly?

Think about how you can incorporate those things that refuel you in small pieces. Maybe that looks like taking a walk for a few minutes each day to get some time to unwind and re-settle your mind. Maybe that looks like a warm bath or a warm cup of tea and a good book before bed. Maybe that's taking time to play games with your kids. Maybe it's sharing three things you were grateful for today with your spouse at dinner.

Set aside time once a week, once a month, once a quarter to specifically nurture your soul. I have a friend who specifically finds activities in these increments to feed her soul. That might be a weekly coffee date or phone call with someone, a monthly massage, and a quarterly day of retreat. This can keep us looking forward to the next event, as well as keep us motivated between them.

Mindfulness

Mindfulness can help us process our trauma, reset our reactions, and lead us in chaotic situations. Mindfulness is focusing your awareness on the present moment. You're actively attentive to the present, observing your thoughts and feelings, without judging them as good or bad.

Being aware of the present can prevent us from focusing on the past or worrying about the future. Learning how to center ourselves daily will help us become less triggered by the situation around us. It also gives us tools to re-center when we are triggered.

This can take many forms. It can be taking a silent walk each day where you mute your phone, don't listen to music or a podcast, and don't talk to anyone. Just observe what's around you and observe what emotions come up in the silence. Don't judge what comes up, just listen to yourself and then allow yourself to let it go.

It can take a bit of getting used to if you're addicted to distracting yourself with busyness and noise. It's hard to slow down and hear our emotions. We might be so used to not listening to the quiet that we have to practice.

Meditation is another great mindfulness practice. I know sometimes we can be hesitant about meditation, but Scripture encourages us to meditate on God's Word and let it soak into our hearts to help us understand the meaning and how to apply it to our lives. You can also find a guided meditation from someone else that can help you focus on gratefulness.

For me, one of the best mindfulness practices is taking time in nature and being struck by the wonder of God's creation. For me, this looks like taking a walk or going on a hike in the woods. For you this might be finding your favorite bench in a park or a garden, or enjoying the quiet while sitting in your own backyard. Take the time to take it in and just relax, be aware of your surroundings and what your heart says to you in those moments.

My other favorite mindfulness practice is journaling. This allows me to process what emotions came up during the day and to re-center my perspective. Sometimes just getting it out on paper can release all those pent-up emotions. I often feel like I've talked it over with a good friend after journaling. But often it helps me let go of those feelings and gives me the ability to move forward with more peace.

A gratitude practice can be part of journaling or meditation. You can think of three people or items you're grateful for when you first wake up and before you go to sleep at night. Start with the small things. You're happy you woke up today, you're thankful you have a roof over your head, you're glad you have God in your life. Your list will expand the more you practice.

Keep in mind the messages you're telling yourself. We talked about it in chapter four, but it applies to all areas of our lives. The words we tell ourselves matter. How we speak to ourselves matters. Pause if you hear a negative message reel playing in your mind. Commit to speaking positive, encouraging beliefs over yourself at every opportunity.

Remember, no judgment. Feelings are feelings. You can accept your feelings as just feelings, not good or bad feelings. You can forgive yourself for how you're feeling if you need to. You can forgive others who have hurt you. You can accept that other people have been hurt too and maybe they haven't learned how to process their emotions yet.

Making a daily routine out of your mindfulness practice is key. It can be very helpful in your day-to-day ability to cope with daily stressors, as well as your long-term ability to handle your emotions. Personally, I like to start my day with devotions, then spend some time cuddling my kitties and having a cup of tea. Some mornings I journal. Then I spend some time in prayer to make sure my heart is aligned with God's heart before I start my day.

Sensing our Limits

Mindfulness can help us get better in tune with our emotions, which in turn will help us to be more aware when we're hitting our limits. For many of us who survived trauma, we've learned how to stuff down our emotions and put on a happy face for those around us, not allowing ourselves to acknowledge how we're feeling in the moment.

By not acknowledging our feelings, we've also gotten out of tune with the signs that we're getting overwhelmed. We just keep stuffing those emotions until it feels unbearable and then we blow up on those around us. There is a better way.

If we're going to successfully lead those around us, we can't be an emotional robot most days, then a ticking time bomb that will go off when we least expect it. We can equip ourselves better than that with some practice.

First, we have to learn what our emotions are. If you've been stuffing them for years, you may not recognize them for what they are. Take some time to define what you're feeling. If your heart starts racing or you get a sick feeling in your stomach, your body is sensing that something is wrong in the situation, or someone is pushing on an emotion that's triggering you.

That's okay. You may not need to react to the current situation, but you can start to recognize it's something your body recognizes as a threat based on something in your past. It can also be a good warning indicator that you might need to change your situation.

Take for example a situation where you have a nervous feeling in your stomach, either your stomach is tied in knots or just aches. Or your shoulders start tensing up. What's driving that emotion for you? Is there a tone in someone's voice that you're dealing with that has set you on edge? What does it remind you of? Is that true in this scenario? Is the edge in someone's voice because they are trying to be authoritative over you, or is it a cultural norm for them that doesn't mean anything?

Or it could be a sign that you're sensing manipulation in their tactics because your body recognizes it from your history. You have to evaluate the truth of the situation and make an educated response. You can ask someone what they mean or where they're coming from to help give you more perspective.

Does someone telling you what you "should" do immediately set you on edge and make you not want to listen to their advice? This is an area where you can likely communicate with them that their approach is triggering. You may be willing to hear their ideas if they ask if they can offer a suggestion and let you respond whether you're open to hearing it before they tell you.

In these situations, it's key to ask more questions to understand what's driving the other person in the conversation. Getting clarity on where they're coming from can help you evaluate if your history is triggering you, if they're triggering you, or it's some of both.

Then you have to be willing to handle what the situation calls for. You might need to take a minute and some deep breaths before you're in a place where you can hear from this person. You may need to ask them to change their approach. You may need to walk away from the situation. Or you may need to set a boundary to ensure your own health.

Boundaries

What do healthy boundaries look like? Often people confuse boundaries with trying to control the other person or change their actions or responses in a situation. The trouble is, we can't actually control other people. The only person we have control over is ourselves. Setting a boundary is about where we reach our limits on how well we can tolerate a situation.

Easier boundaries might look like redirecting or walking away from a gossip session at work. Or it could be the hard boundaries where you have to go "no contact" with someone who's hurt you for a while until you can handle the emotions that come up. And it's okay if "no contact" is the only position you can take long-term with some people in your life.

As a trauma survivor, setting boundaries can seem impossible. If we grew up with someone who took advantage of us, we didn't learn good boundaries as children. We may have been taught that our needs were subservient to others' needs, so standing up for ourselves can feel foreign. We carry those beliefs into our adult lives until we learn to operate differently.

Practice with the small things. Set a boundary with yourself to allow yourself twenty minutes in a good book before you go to bed to help you unwind. Make time for that in your evening.

Set a boundary with a friend who seems to disrespect your time by setting an appointment after your usual phone call or coffee date, so you have a reason to leave the conversation that you don't have to feel guilty about.

Boundaries can also be about what you allow in your life outside of relationships. You can set a boundary that you won't watch certain shows that trigger you or encourage bad habits. You can set a boundary for how much social media content you allow too. It's okay to set a limit that allows you be able to operate in a healthier frame of reference. Ask friends to respect that you may not be up for talking about the news today if there's already enough stress in your life.

It's hard for me when I have to tell someone no or I won't do something with them because I need to honor the priorities God has asked me to honor. I hate disappointing people; I feel guilty for not doing what they want. I feel like I'm letting everyone down. In my own mind I assume they're hurt and will be mad at me.

While I may occasionally be letting them down, more often I'm letting myself down. I have to remember I'm either prioritizing the things God wants me to work on, or prioritizing the things I need to work on for my own mental health; I'm not trying to hurt someone else. Then I can reframe my focus and my energy in the right direction.

People may or may not understand your reasoning. I often really want to try to explain it to them because I feel like then they will understand that I'm not trying to be hurtful. Honestly it doesn't matter how they feel about your boundary, it's yours to make. We just have to remember to communicate our boundaries with kindness and respect.

We also talked about what boundaries in leadership look like in chapter 6 as we discussed courage. Boundaries for your team help set expectations and can mold the culture you're operating in. This applies to any organization or team you're involved in.

Disciplining our Minds

We also need to be careful to discipline our own minds. God asks us to be diligent about how we fill our minds and rein ourselves in when we spiral out of control. We discipline our bodies by eating healthy foods and exercising, but are we paying attention to what fills our minds?

We often worry over our days, how our kids will turn out, how we will provide for ourselves, or how and when disaster will strike. For trauma survivors we have been taught to be on guard for someone's emotions to blow up or the next problem to fix so someone doesn't get angry. That's not where God wants us to focus.

Let's look at some examples of where we should keep our focus.

Mt. 6:25-27, 31-33: [25] *"That is why I tell you not to*

> *worry about everyday life—whether you have enough food and drink, or enough clothes to wear. Isn't life more than food, and your body more than clothing?* **26** *Look at the birds. They don't plant or harvest or store food in barns, for your heavenly Father feeds them. And aren't you far more valuable to him than they are?* **27** *Can all your worries add a single moment to your life?* . . . **31** *So don't worry about these things, saying, 'What will we eat? What will we drink? What will we wear?'* **32** *These things dominate the thoughts of unbelievers, but your heavenly Father already knows all your needs.* **33** *Seek the Kingdom of God above all else, and live righteously, and he will give you everything you need."*

And 2 Ti. 1:7 says this: *"For God has not given us a spirit of fear and timidity, but of power, love, and self-discipline."*

God asks us to seek his kingdom above all else so we can live righteously. He also did not want us to live in fear, but instead gave us a spirit of power, love, and self-discipline. So we know we're capable of being disciplined.

Maybe the problem is, we need to understand HOW to be self-disciplined. Self-discipline can look a lot like healthy boundaries for myself. What things do I want to focus on? What am I filling my mind with? Do I spend time listening to worship music, or do I call a friend to complain about my frustrations? Am I reading God's Word, or do I spend all my time reading romances or fantasy so I can escape my current circumstances?

This is about your health and your growth. It's like all other habits. It takes time to start them and stay consistent with them until they're formed. You get to choose where you want to invest your energy and spend your time so that you become the person you want to be.

Create a Support Network

When we look at our overall health, we also need to remember that we need other people. Honestly, I used to dream of retiring to a semi-remote cabin in the woods. I thought I would do great as a semi-recluse, spending time writing, hiking, and enjoying nature.

Then I landed in a house on thirty acres of forest during the COVID pandemic, in a community where I didn't know anyone. On my own I got lonely and spiraled into depression. I began to realize how much I needed other people in my life. In the interim, I set up routine calls with girlfriends to help me maintain my sanity. They were my lifeline during that time.

When I uprooted my life and started anew again in a town where I knew no one, and was far away from my family, I committed to making friends and getting involved in the community. I knew for my own health, it was nonnegotiable to establish a new network.

I kept my network of girlfriends to talk to throughout the transitions as well. But I got to know my neighbors, I established myself in a church and got involved in my community. It didn't happen overnight, but a year of investing paid off.

Three years down the road, I know I'm part of a network of friends and adopted family who watch out for me and care for me. They invest in my heart and support my dreams. God is so gracious. He continues to bring people into my path who are "my tribe."

Moving Into Success as a Leader

We're all on a journey in our lives. We still want to learn and improve, to have meaning in our lives. To have gotten this far in your journey you've been willing to do the hard work to survive or get out of your traumatic past. You've also done the work to grasp your healing.

Now you want to see how you can impact for good in others' lives. That's remarkable! I'm proud of you for being willing to seek more in your life and to allow God to unfold the good out of your experiences.

You're setting yourself up for success as a leader. By putting daily practices into place, you're giving yourself the practices for more acceptance in your life, which will also give you more peace. You're more prepared to handle other people and able to set boundaries where you need to for your own health.

You'll also be able to share these practices with your team, even incorporate them into your language and meetings as a team. This can help impact how you relate to each other as a team, what your culture looks like, and how you can be more effective in making decisions.

Taking the time for your own mindfulness will give you greater capacity to hear your team's input without dismissing it, being able to evaluate it for its merits. This respect and willingness to listen will pay dividends in how your team interacts.

Next let's look at who we want to be as leaders. Let's evaluate what kind of leader we want to be by looking at what we respect most in other leaders. Then let's utilize those boundaries and learn to trust other people. By learning to delegate, you'll be more effective as a leader and an organization.

Chapter 10
Learning to Lead

My first manager is still my favorite. Janie was a fireball. She loved fiercely and wholeheartedly. She worked tirelessly and didn't complain and would turn the conversation to service if anyone started to whine. She was great at explaining a task to you and doing it beside you until you were comfortable. Then she would trust you to do it on your own.

I still remember making big batches of caramel corn with her. It was my first summer in a commercial kitchen and I was getting used to cooking for 100-125 instead of for four. The first time she stayed in the kitchen in the afternoon and taught me how to make the caramel, and then quickly get it on the popcorn while it was foaming.

Once I was comfortable with the process, she would leave me to make it on my own but would be down the hall resting if I needed her. As the summer went on, she'd let me handle the evening snacks on my own, making them in the afternoon and serving them in the evenings. I loved that she taught me and then handed over responsibility as soon as I was ready.

She was safety conscious. She'd send you home to change if you didn't wear close-toed shoes in the kitchen. She wanted us to leave a good impression on our guests, so we were taught to always be polite, kind, and helpful. She expected a lot of her team and would let you know if you weren't meeting expectations, but in a kind way, never shaming you.

But I was most struck by the strong Christian woman she was. She always asked people about what they were learning in their lives. She would pray with those who were struggling. She would speak up in staff Bible studies about what she was learning. She would talk about her walk with God comfortably.

She also taught me that work and leading can be done in an authentic manner, that includes your faith, and you can still have fun. There was a sign in her kitchen that said 'demaphlagie spoken here'. Demaphlagie didn't have a specific meaning, it was a representation of any word she couldn't think of thanks to peri-menopausal brain fog. She was often down for a good prank as well. I loved that she didn't take herself too seriously.

What a Leader Looks Like

Leadership may sound new to you, so I want to start out with a couple of items key to your success as a leader. Leading by example has always been the most authentic form of leadership I've experienced.

Who do you want to be when you grow up? That picture has likely changed from who we idolized as kids or teenagers to who we look up to today. But for some of us, there are similarities to who we look up to throughout our lives. What characteristics do these people have that you admire?

How do you start acting like that person? What would someone who has achieved the goal you set be focusing their mind on? Looking at others as an example of how to achieve something we want to achieve is healthy.

Get to know their story. Look at their struggles and how they solved them. Take what they learned and apply it to your scenario. It can save you a lot of time instead of treating everything you face as unique. Usually we can find something similar in another person's experiences.

Help yourself stay open to what people around you have experienced in their lives. Be willing to have the conversation, be willing to open up to other people. This can expand your viewpoint and broaden your knowledge.

When I look at the first women who were leaders in my life, there are some characteristics they had in common. They were kind and they cared about people. They approached leadership with a servant's heart. At the same time, they were strong women who rarely complained and who could say no kindly when they needed to.

They were hardworking. But they did work they loved, and their love showed through in what they did or made. They set high expectations for themselves and expected others to follow those standards as well. They operated in utmost integrity, always. They were authentic people who didn't put on a false front or try to appear different from who they were in their daily lives.

They were submitted to God in their lives and in their leadership.

They started their mornings with prayer, and they were willing to talk about what God was teaching them in their lives. They understood the heart of the ministry and kept focused on how they could best serve the ministry.

These women motivated me to keep my heart focused on the right places. They gave me great examples of how to lead people well. They taught me how to set expectations and hold people accountable, but all in a loving manner.

Keys to Leadership

1. Submitted to God first

Priorities matter. When you're evaluating how you want to impact others, you're going to define what's most important and what's secondary. At the same time, you have to decide where this work (organization, ministry, business, etc.) fits in your personal priorities. That will help you define how much time and energy you have to give, and where you can start.

The ability to impact people comes primarily from the heart, in this case, your heart. In order to keep your focus on the best ways to pursue your impact, you need to ensure you're aligned with what God's asking you to do. Which means you will need to take the time to listen to his voice and hear his directions.

This goes back to the practices you put in place in your daily life that we talked about in the last chapter. Are you starting your mornings with prayer and time in God's Word, so you can hear where he is leading your heart? It can be super easy to get overwhelmed with everything you're trying to do to start something new, but it's key that you take the time to remain centered in him, so your focus is on where he's leading you.

The other key here is to listen to his way and his timing. Opening your heart to fully submitted leadership. Remember how I talked about God only giving us the vision and the first steps because we'd try to run on our own if we knew the answers? This is where that gets put into practice every day. Spending time communing with him to ensure we aren't running out ahead of him.

2. Leading by example

I appreciate leaders who are willing to work beside me and understand the effort I'm putting in. It's also great that they are well-equipped to advise me when issues come up because they fully understand the intricacies of the job.

But it's key that they earned my respect by being able to teach me and show me what to do. Managers who relied on me to do the work but who couldn't answer my questions when issues arose did not earn my respect. I think that's a key difference to note, one I saw as a leader, one I saw as merely my supervisor.

Not often do we have people who know exactly how to do the job we're asking of them in the way that works best with our organization. Everyone needs some teaching and training, even if it's predominantly values and culture instead of a skill set. The more you can show them yourself, the more they will believe in you, and they'll also gain a deeper understanding of what your goals and intentions are as you work together.

Here's where you also want to keep in mind the great characteristics you've learned in your life. Your team has not had your same experiences, and they may not have learned the same leadership values you have. But you can teach them by demonstrating why those values are important on a daily basis and give them examples to see why it matters in how it influences other people or makes them feel.

3. **Authentic leadership**

To be the leader we admire, we have to imitate that person in truth. Our actions and our appearance have to align. We have to ***be*** the leader we want to be, not just try to look like the leader we want to be.

People can only believe in us if we're authentic. Our depth of character is what will draw people to us. The more we lead from an authentic place of compassion and caring for those we want to serve, the more effective we will be.

This also flows into how we encourage our team. Genuine praise and admiration speak volumes over fluffy words that feel generic or learned. Thanking our team for what they're doing and showing them how they're bringing the desired results will continue to motivate them.

One of the biggest lessons I learned early on working in commercial kitchens was to get in the mix. I remember one particular evening when the dishwashing crew really wanted to go to the church service that night, and they had intentionally come in early to clear out any dishes they could ahead of time. They ate dinner quickly, and as soon as the dishes came in, they cleared them as fast as they could.

The people receiving the plates had a great system going and kept the dishwasher running as fast as possible. On the other side of the room, another person was working the pans. I stepped in beside them and helped them get through the pans more quickly as well.

They were very surprised that I would step in and help them. When it was nearly time for service, I sent them on their way and told them I would finish that evening. They were surprised and very appreciative and willing to take me up on the offer.

It completely drove the direction of my leadership style. Rather than being a leader who gives direction, delegates everything, and is unwilling to get my hands dirty, I was someone who would step beside the team in the hard jobs. I would even finish for them when they'd put in a lot of effort and had something else they really wanted to do.

I rewarded their motivation and effort, and I showed them that I wasn't above them just because I had more expertise. It felt good to know that I was still part of the team even while I led them.

4. Vulnerability as a leader

Our patterns of shame may keep us from feeling safe to be vulnerable as a leader. We have to be willing to step out of the old beliefs and into our new beliefs, where we know it's okay to be honest and real with people in our lives. We don't have to be perfect to earn respect. We'll earn respect faster by our willingness to live in our truth with an open heart.

Vulnerability as a leader can be hard to demonstrate. In my college years, I was taught not to be friends with my employees. I was told I couldn't manage them unless I kept a professional distance. There's good advice in those words, but the trouble is that logic hurts my heart. I wanted to be more open and honest with my team.

I was fortunate in my first career to experience a different kind of leadership than the world normally models as successful. Here it was demonstrated to me that you could be open and vulnerable and be friendly with your team and still earn their respect. We could pray together, worship together, and still work together. This can be well modeled inside a ministry but also works in the public sector.

I'm still open and vulnerable with my employees and colleagues. Standing up for my team and being honest when I don't have it all together has strongly increased the loyalty in my team. Knowing we have each other's backs is a much better dynamic than competing against each other.

With these principles in mind, I hope you're starting to picture who you want to be as a leader. Now let's look at a practical example that you'll need to be successful as a leader, learning how to delegate.

Learning to Delegate

We can have the best plans and intentions, but then we have to account for real-life scenarios. Let's be honest, often the hardest part of being a leader is learning how to work with others and learning how to give up control of some things while still maintaining the desired result. I know my standard response used to be to take things on myself because I know what to expect. The trouble is, I will also wear myself out with this pattern.

I had learned in both my growing-up years, and within my marriage, the wrong way to handle difficulties. I had seen the impact of depending on someone and then having them be irresponsible. I didn't have a role where I felt I could define consequences for their actions. So, my response was to take everything on myself and not trust them to help me.

But I had a very different experience early in my career. When I first started managing other people, I still took on too much of the workload myself, not wanting to overload anyone else, or seem like I was just "managing" them without being willing to contribute myself.

What I learned over time was how much freedom I gained by learning to delegate. I could focus on the tasks I was good at or that needed my expertise and allow others to do the other tasks I had either already taught them, or they already knew how to do. This was amazing!

Suddenly my productivity level could increase because I had a crew of people working towards the same goal in an organized fashion, versus me struggling to cover everything by myself. This was something I needed to learn to survive in my first jobs. We had tight deadlines several times a day, and being able to delegate and depend on others was key to success.

What Keeps Us from Delegating to Others?

At the root of it, our lack of ability to delegate stems from three sources: our desire for perfection, our need for validation through performance recognition, and our lack of trust. Let's look at each.

First, many of us who have experienced trauma are now driven to perfectionism. It's a coping mechanism we learned in childhood. If we can take care of everything and make sure no one gets upset, then we can, for the moment, prevent another emotional outburst, angry argument, or avoid the blame for someone else's toxic behavior. We believe our efforts keep the peace, and emotionally we want to maintain peace at all costs. We fight so hard to maintain complete control over the scenario that we can't imagine trusting anyone else to take care of it for us.

Second, being raised in trauma can also drive us to seek our validation through performance. We weren't valued as individuals; we were valued for what we brought to the family or how we added value for the narcissist. The only way we could earn favorable attention was through positive performance that reflected well on our parents or family.

We can often mistake this performance reward for love, since we were not shown what real love was if we grew up in homes with trauma. The only thing near to love we felt was performance recognition, so we still crave it until we've learned to replace that with unconditional love. While it may be subconscious, we are still striving for that validation to soothe our inner child's soul. We're still looking for our parents' approval, even when they are unable to give it to us.

Third, we learned not to trust others because they either failed us and upset the model where we took care of everything to avoid the abuser's wrath, or they turned on us and degraded and blamed us when they didn't complete their own responsibilities. Either case leaves us to bear the responsibility on our own and be forced to answer for someone else's mistakes. Both perfectionism and looking for performance validation have at their root a lack of trust.

Trust comes down to how much we trust ourselves and how much we trust God. Trauma leaves us feeling we can't trust anyone, including ourselves. If we were trustworthy, we would have seen the issues we faced coming sooner and been able to handle them differently. While this is a crazy untruth, it can be part of our subconscious beliefs.

We also don't trust God because he didn't rescue us from our trauma, or at least not completely. If he is all knowing and all seeing, why did he allow what happened to us? It's a subconscious belief we have to replace with the truth of his Word deep in our hearts before we can reconcile how this belief has been messing with our lives up to this point.

God does allow consequences for our sin and for sin in the lives of people around us, which may impact us as well. While it may not feel fair, the reality is that there are consequences for our sin. It can be especially hard to accept consequences after we are repentant for what we've done. We hope that he will also erase the consequences at the time of our repentance and forgiveness. God does wash away the debt of our sin, but he does not always wash away the consequences in this lifetime, only in eternity.

We have to learn to trust that he knows the whole story and he has our good in mind. It can be hard for us to trust our future to his plans when we can't see where he's leading us. But his Word says he does:

- Pr. 3:5-6 *"Trust in the Lord with all your heart; do not depend on your own understanding. Seek his will in all you do, and he will show you which path to take."*

- Ro. 8:28 *"And we know that God causes everything to work together for the good of those who love God and are called according to his purpose for them."*

That's the point: it requires us to trust.

We're still left with the fallout from our lack of trust until we've healed our emotions and learned new patterns. We may still want everything to turn out "just right," and we still want people to like and appreciate us. But if we want to accomplish the goals God has for our lives, we need to change our focus from our former patterns to how we can achieve the goals he has for us.

We have to step into trusting ourselves and trusting other people. So how do we do that? We get to learn to come with open hands and give others a chance to thrive under our leadership at the same time. Let's talk about what that looks like.

How to Delegate

We want to change our former patterns. Let's talk about how to do this practically.

1. **Figure out where your strengths are and where you are less efficient.**

Take the time to do an honest assessment of yourself. Where do you have skills, talents, and abilities? Where are you very efficient at something, or what comes easily to you? What natural abilities make you so great at it?

Also be honest with yourself about where you don't have strengths, where you would be more effective to have someone help you. It's not a weakness to recognize you're not good at everything. It's honesty.

2. Hire good people who have the skills that complement you.

Once you've evaluated your own strengths and weaknesses, look for where you can use the most help. Where are the gaps in your skill set that having a teammate would benefit you? Define what that need is and what you're looking for in an employee.

It's important to hire the right people. Look for people who have those skills you need, but it's also very important that the people you hire have the same values you have for your organization. Your dream is your child, be cognizant that you trust your employees with your dream.

3. Define clear expectations for others and give them the ability to ask specific questions while they're learning.

Documented, clear expectations can solve many problems, as well as give you a line to measure against when issues arise. Putting it down in writing for both people to absorb and refer to is helpful.

Think about your values and goals as an organization and put those in writing. But also think about where you can document processes so that you can set a standard expectation for how you want tasks accomplished. Give employees checklists to refer to, so processes feel more routine. This can also help alleviate mistakes when we're tired.

Give employees ample opportunities to ask questions along the way. Walk them through the process, then have them do it themselves with you nearby so they can confer with you when they need clarification. Then allow them to perform the task on their own without your help and give them feedback on the results.

4. Set a timeframe for getting up to speed.

Give the person who's learning time to get up to speed. Also, set an expectation of when you want them to be able to do the job on their own, so they know what they're working towards. Have regular check-ins along the way.

This may be a day-to-day occurrence if you're working closely together, but if not, make sure to schedule time for this to ensure their success. Let them voice to you if they can't meet that expectation and what they need to be successful.

5. Be willing to let people go if they don't meet your expectations.

Letting people go is a tough line to hold to but will help you be so much more effective in the long run. You have to be willing to hold the boundary you've set, otherwise people will push your boundaries again and again.

Life has consequences. It's good to have standards you expect, and employment comes with expectations for results. If, after retraining or clarifying expectations, they can't be met, it's okay to recognize this isn't a good fit.

6. Start trusting your team with more.

Once someone has met your initial goals for them, continue to stretch them. Continue to add more items to their responsibility list and see how they perform. Check in with them to ensure they're not taking on more than they can handle.

See if there are tasks they can hand off to someone else as well, if you see they're excelling. The more you can trust them to take on additional responsibilities, the more time it can give you for your own responsibilities or to focus on other areas in the organization where you're needed.

7. Encourage them to succeed/empower them.

People love positive feedback, and we give it too sparingly. Keep noticing how well they are doing with increasing responsibilities and let them know you notice. Find what empowers and motivates your team and use those means to praise them.

8. Make it worth their while.

Reward people for positive behavior. This can take the form of recognition, of more freedom in their decisions. It could look like incentives or a stake in the business. You get to decide how, but make sure it fits the person you're motivating.

9. Keep practicing trust.

Take the next steps forward for you as well. Allow more people to prove to you they are trustworthy. Take the opportunity to trust more people. At the same time, lean into God more. Learn how to trust him with your life and with your decisions. He knows your heart, you can trust him with it.

Set yourself up for success as a leader. Let go of what's been holding you back and keeping you from trusting yourself and trusting others. Give it up to God and allow him to lead you. He'll show you the right people, and He'll help you learn to trust them. And you know from everything you've learned where to trust your intuition. Leaning into God and trusting his leading will give you intuition that's led by the Spirit.

You have gifts you were meant to share with the world, and you can be an effective leader. Let's step into what that looks like for you!

Chapter 11
The New You as a Leader

How are you feeling? We've looked at our beliefs together and begun reframing those based on the truth of God's word. We looked at seven different leadership traits together to help you see the strength you gained through your experiences. I bet there are even more traits you've thought of as you've evaluated your stories as you've listened to some of mine.

Are you excited to start stepping into a leadership role? Maybe you're still tentative, still working on absorbing what we've been talking about. I understand. It can be a lot to take in. But I want you to know it's worth it.

It's all been worth it. I never thought I would be able to say that. In the many dark nights of the soul along the way, I lost hope so many times. I blamed God for everything that had happened, and I lashed out in anger against him for allowing trauma in my life.

Why couldn't it have been easier? Why did I have to go through things that seemed harder than most people around me? Some moments I believed I must have done something wrong that I didn't even remember I was being punished for.

None of that was true. That was a lot of lies the devil put in my mind to keep me from healing and to keep me from moving forward. A whole lot of malarkey that kept me lost for a while.

Thankfully God knew and he kept reaching out for me, even when I chose to refuse him.

> What I couldn't see then was that the depth of my pain would turn into a depth of relationship with him. That's where I actually won in the process.

By turning back and leaning into him, I finally became that Christian with a depth of soul and breadth of experience that was authentic. I had stepped forward from my fluffy, surface-level, never-been-challenged beliefs into real, hard-earned faith. Finally, truly knowing God was the one person I could count on in the midst of everything else.

When I look back at some of the things I wrote in my 20s, I can see the depth of pain and confusion I had experienced, even though in hindsight that was not the worst of it. But my level of faith was shallow. I wanted to know God, but I didn't know yet how to trust him.

I'm not saying I needed to experience the amount of complex trauma I did to get to where I am. But it did leave me a very sweet gift for having experienced it. Clawing my way into my healing taught me to lean into Jesus, because he can be trusted. The sweetest relationship I could ask for is with the Savior I can lean on for everything.

That's where I want you to see yourself as well. Fully, abundantly trusting in the God who brought you through the long, dark nights and healed you. You had to put in the hard work, but he brought you here.

God is writing his story in us to share with others. The stories of our lives are stories he can use to minister to others. While we see them as areas we've failed or disappointed him, instead he gave us a gift to be able to relate to others, to open a door from our life experiences into theirs, a way to communicate with someone who is one step behind us on the journey.

Believing in Your Ability to Lead Others

Leadership begins with you believing in yourself. Take in the words from the Bible and let them soak into your soul. Take the time to study the verses I've offered in earlier chapters and hear God speak over your life. Take some time to reflect on the skills you've learned along the way. Give yourself grace.

Let go of the naysayers in your head. I understand this can be difficult, especially if it's what you've been taught for a long time. Learning to take small steps forward and changing the narrative in your mind are essential skills.

You have the ability. You know it in your soul. Now you need to start taking action. Action is key to letting go of your old beliefs. Taking action will actually quiet the overwhelm you're feeling.

Just getting started is the key. Taking small steps every day will help you make progress. Making progress will give you hope. Hope is what sustains us and motivates us.

We've spent the last several chapters on reframing your experiences into leadership skills. Changing your beliefs and your thinking is the key to allowing yourself to become the leader you've envisioned.

Grasping Your Vision and Sharing it

God has given you a specific story, a specific set of experiences, so that you can reach people who can relate to what you've been through. Start thinking about what parts of your story other people have also been through. Where are the specific areas of need that you have a heart for?

Think about what you've been through, the hard times you learned to survive and become stronger through. Are there people around you who could benefit from your experiences and what you learned?

Sometimes you're not sure you know the answer, and that's okay. It's a great place to experiment from. You can try helping organizations or serving in new areas and see how it feels. Does it suit you? Does it reach your heart? If not, it's okay to try something else.

Spend a lot of time on your knees. Ask God to bring you an opportunity. Open your heart and mind to what God has for you. It doesn't always look like we'd expect. And God doesn't tell us the whole story up front. He wants us to lean on him all along the way.

If he told us everything up front, you know our silly human hearts would say, "Thanks God! I've got this from here!" Which isn't at all how he wants our relationship to be.

> He's the best, wisest, and most level-headed business partner we could ask for. We can ask him anything along the way.

He sees where we're going, and he knows our hearts would get caught up in the personal glory rather than staying next to him. So he walks beside us all along the way.

What is on your heart the most? Are there certain situations you're passionate about helping people out of? Are there causes you strongly believe in and want to support? If money and time were no object, what would you do to improve the world?

Start there. Ask God to open your eyes to the needs around you. Ask him to show you what your heart wants.

This can often be something related to something you've experienced in your own life. God will use your experiences to minister to others. I know it's often not what we choose if we could start over again. But remember this has also become our strength.

Using Your Story to Empower Others

As a leader you can acknowledge what you've learned has given you strength in areas you wouldn't have stepped out in before. Often, we have a heart for teaching others to step forward in the areas where we have learned the most. That's valuable to them as well.

Sometimes the best thing we can be is support to someone around us. To say, "I've walked through this. Today this is really hard, but I want to see you succeed, and I want to help you through it. Because I know you're strong enough to get to the other side."

For many of us we need to expand our definition of leadership. We see leadership as something formal that requires an important title, and likely an organization behind it. But it's more than that. Leadership can take many different forms.

Leadership can look like mentoring other women. It can look like discipling your children. It can be supporting a sister through a tough time, helping her see the path out of her situation.

It can also be leading a group. It can be teaching others a skill set you have. It can look like taking people into your home and giving them an opportunity you didn't have. It can be standing up for others in tough situations.

It can also look like some of the traditional definitions of leadership—teaching, organizing events, and leading a group of colleagues through projects. It's all of these things. You get to define how you want it to look for you.

You can utilize the discernment you've learned to help coach and guide your teenagers through the struggles they're having with relationships. You can use the compassion you've learned to help you in dealing with the relationships in your life—whether that's colleagues at work, your parents, or your friends. You can model courage to your children and to peers you're mentoring.

If you're leading an organization today, you can use your compassion to help you understand when employees are struggling with an issue at home that may impact their concentration at work. You can utilize your ability to pivot to help you make better business decisions. You can persist for the goals you want to accomplish in your personal life or with a team. You can continue to learn how to nurture your inner health so you continue to lead from the best version of yourself.

Start with a few people or a small organization. See where you can make an impact. Watch to see what brings you joy and focus on that. God may grow your gifting faster than you expected. By all means, celebrate that when it comes! Lean into God's timing for the best results.

Let your passion guide you for your purpose. There are people you want to help, who you want to help grow. Your strength comes from what you've learned. Take that strength into leading others.

Moving Forward

Many of you may feel inadequately equipped for this journey. This is where you have to remember to lean into God's strength instead of your own. Step out in fear and faith. You can do this! And I'm right here beside you, cheering you on and encouraging you.

Picture yourself as the leader you want to be. Really imagine it. Is there someone you think of that you want to be like? See yourself as that person. How would you act as that person? What would you be doing already? How would you be doing it?

If you can envision what it will look like, then you can set yourself up to work towards that. Take that dream and then walk through the steps to get there. Then break down each of those steps into smaller, more manageable pieces.

Visualize yourself taking that small step and achieving that first goal. This tricks your brain into setting you up for success. Just visualizing the end goal won't get you there. You have to see the steps on the path, and you need to visualize yourself completing the next step.

The key is to visualize yourself not just in success but also in the hard days. You have to see yourself running in the rain every day instead of just seeing yourself winning a race. Finishing the race in the time you've set is a great goal, but if you only visualize the end of the race versus visualizing how you practice running every day, you won't know how to get there. (Robbins, 2021)[1]

Take the first step and start working towards it, a little bit every day if you can. Taking a few minutes to make progress will reap rewards faster than you realize. You'll see yourself making progress and that will motivate you to keep going. Often you're so excited

---

1. Robbins, M. (2021). The High 5 Habit. In M. Robbins, *The High 5 Habit* (pp. 195-197). Carlsbad, CA: Hayhouse Inc.

with your progress that your motivation keeps you moving.

Also think about the attitude you would have if you were already leading where you want to lead. You would have such confidence in your abilities because you're successful at it. That's where you're headed, so believe in it today and act that way already.

Let's take an example. I wanted to be an author. First, I had to believe I had something worth sharing with the world. That took some time for me to reframe my own beliefs. I spent time in God's Word, poring over the words where he tells me he loves me, where he created my inner being before I was born into the world. (Ps. 139)

I had to remember the fact that he wouldn't change anything about me. He saw my whole story before I was born and knew it would happen this way. He doesn't blame me or hold against me my actions if I've asked for forgiveness. He sees me for exactly who I am and loves me completely.

Only when I truly believed his words could I live my life authentically. He helped me sort out the untruths from the truth. He taught me to trust in his Spirit to lead my heart to discern correctly. I don't get it right on my own. I had to lean into him to stay attuned to his voice and his leading; that's something that I still have to do daily.

Learning to forgive others and myself taught me to have compassion for those around me who are struggling, even for those who had hurt me. I'm much faster to forgive myself and others than I used to be, because I've learned that holding on to my emotions and anger really only hurts me.

I learned to have a voice. I learned to ask the questions. I learned to put my dreams out in the world and speak them to close friends around me. It took an immense amount of courage to share my dreams, but I found sharing them with trusted friends helped encourage me and keep me motivated. Keeping it to myself only let the naysayers in my head have more power than they deserved.

Voicing my dreams to a larger audience was super empowering. Understandably this needs to be with people who are in your corner. But voicing my book theory to other writers was the best step I could have taken. Over and over, I was met with encouragement.

I learned I could adapt. There didn't need to be shame attached to failure. Failure is part of the learning process. Getting back up and trying again was something I had done so many times in life. I had to give myself the grace and compassion to fail. I had to accept failure as part of the learning curve and part of the process rather than as a defeat.

Originally, I took on what was too much for one book, unsure of how to break it down. Here's where I needed help from experts. Being able to talk through the ideas with an editor helped me center on what my main message was and define my audience. Over time I narrowed the focus down to a manageable topic for one book.

Then I had to break that topic down into chapters. Writing a whole book felt overwhelming. But writing a chapter, or even a couple points within a chapter, sounded plausible. Then when I had one chapter, I could do the next one. I had to convince myself I was just writing a few pages on a topic I was familiar with.

I had pictured writing as many words flowing out of me on inspired days. I set aside Saturdays when I could make huge progress. I set up a clean office or dining room table, and I had candles and tea and fun snacks. I was ready for this!

But I found myself easily distracted. I would get sidelined by the voices in my head that discouraged me. I would start another load of laundry and get a fresh cup of tea. At the end of the day, I would have words, but often it felt more like journaling than something anyone would want to read. (Just a side note, often journaling is what sparks the ideas for a chapter, so don't discount that.)

Reality looks more like 500-1000 words at a time in my pajamas any given day before I rush off to the rest of my day. Consistency as many days as I could manage was key. The more I stayed in the mental space of writing each day, the less I had to re-center myself on where I was. And the progress, even when slow, was encouraging.

Then I had to persist each day and each week towards the finish line. Some days the words were good, some days there was nothing useful. But I persisted. The more I kept focused on the goal, the clearer the words got. I had to be more patient with myself than I expected. In my mind's eye this was easier and faster than it played out to be.

For me, the daily practices and mindfulness were very helpful. Taking the time in the morning to be in God's Word and in prayer sets my mind on him, and my focus closer to his. Lighting a candle and taking some deep breaths before I started writing helped settle my mind from bouncing around to focusing on my task for today. Ignoring technology and my to-do list for the day until I had taken some time for myself and my goals set the tone for productivity.

I also learned where I needed to ask for help, where I couldn't do everything on my own. I needed a coach to keep me on task and encouraged. I needed someone to ask questions of, bounce ideas off, or to reinvigorate my thinking when I got stuck. An editor and beta readers helped me say what I meant.

My goal came to fruition with the book you're reading now. I'm getting to share a piece of my story and encourage you to look at your story and yourself in a new light. That's amazing! I'm so excited to see this dream come true.

I can also tell you this is step one in a larger picture. The dream I have is to also take this into practical applications. I see myself starting a ministry where I can teach women who have survived trauma how to change their beliefs so they can become leaders in their communities.

I also want to be able to teach them practical skill sets, empower them in their independence, and give them ways to provide for themselves financially. I want to be a supporter of ministries that enable families to own their own homes.

Stay tuned for the next stages of this story. God is working. It doesn't look exactly how expected it, honestly it looks better than I expected. God's fulfilling not just my asks, but also my desires. I continue to stay open to the exact way God will make this happen. But I know he's got it.

Take Your Leadership into Your World

What does leadership look like for you? Where can you start having an impact? What makes your heart soar when you think about it? Let's take a look at some examples together to help spark ideas for where you want to lead.

Let's look first at home. Are you already active in your children or teenagers' lives? If not, can you start teaching them more about your faith and skills that you've learned from your trauma that made you stronger? Do you need to teach them to have compassion for others, and help them understand how to have compassion for themselves? Can you be a role model for them in how you exhibit compassion to your own parents or friends in your life?

Do you have young adults in your household who are taking on their first jobs? Can you help mentor them in how to be better employees and how to take on responsibilities? Can you practice taking on responsibility with them by giving them areas they can control at home?

The workplace may be the more obvious place we think of when we think of leadership. Do you have an opportunity to mentor or coach your colleagues? Can you model compassion in the workplace for them instead of manipulation and control?

What's key is finding where your heart wants to impact people. That's the first item to consider. Often once you listen to your heart, you can see how your background and skills have equipped you. Maybe you already have relationships with people who can help you.

Don't worry about how big or small something is to start. Just look at where you can start. Look around you. Where are you already involved in leadership, or where are you involved in organizations that you would like to take a leadership role in? Or what do you want to get involved in?

Start today. Pick what makes your heart soar and start. I'm a person who has big dreams that can feel impossible. But by starting with the first piece and spending time working towards that every day, I've been able to accomplish goals that once sounded overwhelming. Take the next step forward.

Invite friends on this journey with you. Friends you can talk to, bounce ideas off, and get support from. They may eventually want to join you in your endeavors, but that's not the goal today. Today you need a network to keep you encouraged.

Take hold of your life with both hands. You've been given a gift, and you get to decide how you're going to use it. You've been given more strength than you know with what you've learned up to this point. You've succceded in surviving your trauma and becoming a better and stronger person for it.

No one gets to take more time from you. Now is your time to step into the person you were made to be. This time is your time. Set your heart before you. Where you focus your heart is where you will focus your energy.

You were designed with a purpose. God has laid a promise for good over your life, just as he has mine. I can't wait to see what that looks like! God never goes back on his promises. He will fulfill his promise to you. Ask him today what that promise is over your life and ask him to give you the first details. He will give you the vision. He will point you to the first steps.

Take that step, my friend. I promise you the journey is worth it.

Appendix A

You may have only been told one side of the story. For those of you who are considering whether you have any options to let go of an abusive marriage, I want you to consider some of these verses.

God gives us more freedom in our choices than we often hear from those around us in the church. It's especially hard to face condemnation and rejection from fellow believers. They are the people we want to support us most.

I recognize the Bible doesn't speak specifically about divorce except in the case of adultery, but I would ask you to consider the following verses about how God feels we should relate to and treat each other, and what hurts his heart.

I don't present these as an excuse to take our commitments lightly, but I do believe God allows grace in cases outside of his desires for us. I'm not trying to tell you what the right answer is for your scenario. But I want to lay before you more information so you can take that to God in your wrestling.

Jm. 1:19-20 *"This you know, my beloved brethren. But everyone must be quick to hear, slow to speak and slow to anger; for the anger of man does not achieve the righteousness of God."*

Ps. 11:5 *"The Lord tests the righteous and the wicked, and the one who loves violence His soul hates."*

Ps. 140:12 *"I know that the Lord will maintain the cause of the afflicted and justice for the poor."*

I bring the first several of these specifically to your attention because they talk about anger, wickedness, and violence, which you may be experiencing in your marriage. God hates these things. He does not take lightly those who use these things against his children.

He also is our biggest supporter when we're afflicted or experiencing injustice. He stands beside us and fights for us.

Consider how much God loves you. Below are a few examples.

- Rm. 5:5 *"And this hope will not lead to disappointment. For we know how dearly **God loves us**, because he has given us the Holy Spirit to fill our hearts with his love."*

- 1 Jn. 3:1 *"See how very much our Father **loves us**, for he* *calls us his children, and that is what we are!"*

- 1 Jn. 4:16 *"We know how much **God loves us**, and we have put our trust in his love. God is love, and all who live in love live in God, and God lives in them."*

- Rm. 5:8 *"But **God** showed his great love for **us** by sending Christ to die for **us** while we were still sinners."*

Let's also consider how husbands and wives should love and relate to each other.

> Ep. 5:25-29 *"For husbands, this means love your wives, just as Christ loved the church. He gave up his life for her to make her holy and clean, washed by the cleansing of God's word. He did this to present her to himself as a glorious church without a spot or wrinkle or any other blemish. Instead, she will be holy and without fault. In the same way, husbands ought to love their wives as they love their own bodies. For a man who loves his wife actually shows love for himself. No one hates his own body but feeds and cares for it, just as Christ cares for the church. And we are members of his body."*

We ought to love our spouses more than we love ourselves. We also love and respect ourselves in a healthy way, but not in an arrogant, prideful, overly dominant way. We **love** each other first and care for our partner. If we're not being treated that way, I would question how well we are loved in our relationship.

God doesn't ask us to remain in bondage or abuse. He frees the captives who are enslaved in sin (Is. 61). He wants us to find freedom in him.

Take what's on your heart to God. He's big enough to handle all of it. You can tell him how hurt and angry you are. Then ask him what he wants you to do. Let him guide your path forward.

Acknowledgements

Thank you, Mom and Dad, for always encouraging me to follow my dreams. Thank you to my brother, sister-in-law, nephew and niece for your love, support and encouragement. I love you all!

Thank you, Carla Day, for listening and letting me bounce endless ideas off you. Thank you for always encouraging me in the process.

Thank you, Mikaela Mathews, for all your support and encouragement while I wrote this book. You've been the best coach and editor anyone could ask for! You kept pushing me to continue and got me back on track every time I got derailed along the way. You kept seeing me complete this book on the days I didn't see it.

Thank you, Kathi Gregoire, for always being willing to talk through ideas and continue to encourage me to follow the path God specifically designed for me.

Thank you, Sarah Lamaak, for being my cheerleader and biggest fan throughout this journey. Thank you for welcoming me back as a friend and supporting me through the many pivots over the last few years.

Thank you, Ladies of Lighthouse, for all your prayers over the last three years, it means the world to me how you love me!

Thank you, Jay Loucks, for being an encouraging friend and being willing to support me in seeing this dream come to life.

I appreciate all of you and I couldn't have done this without you!

Let's Stay Connected!

www.fromtraumatoleadership.com

www.instagram.com\fromtraumatoleadership

Coming Soon!

www.auntselenasbakery.com

References

Founder Institute. (2023, April 26). Retrieved from fi.co : https://fi.co/insight/what-pivoting-is-when-to-pivot-and-how-to-pivot-effectively

Holy Bible, New Living Translation, copyright © 1996, 2004, 2015 by Tyndale House Foundation. Used by permission of Carol Stream, Illinois 60188. All rights reserved.

Ryder, G. (2025, February 18). *Psych Central.* Retrieved from https://psychcentral.com/health/what-is-trauma

Robbins, M. (2021). The High 5 Habit. In M. Robbins, *The High 5 Habit* (pp. 195-197). Carlsbad, CA: Hayhouse Inc.

www.ingramcontent.com/pod-product-compliance
Lightning Source LLC
Chambersburg PA
CBHW062214080426
42734CB00010B/1888